W9-BNT-856

Newport, New Hampshire

Prime Ministers

Prime Ministers

Ranking Canada's Leaders

J.L. Granatstein / Norman Hillmer

A Phyllis Bruce Book
HarperCollins*PublishersLtd*

For Robert Bothwell and John English

Photo credits for chapter openings:
p. 15: National Archives of Canada C–7494
p. 29: National Archives of Canada C–4953
p. 37: (clockwise from top left): National Archives of Canada PA–33933, National Archives of Canada C–698, National Archives of Canada C–10109, National Archives of Canada PA–27222
p. 46: National Defence
p. 61: National Archives of Canada PA–28129
p. 75: National Archives of Canada C–691
p. 83: National Archives of Canada C–26989
p. 102: National Archives of Canada
p. 114: National Archives of Canada C–10461
p. 127: National Archives of Canada PA–57930
p. 137: National Archives of Canada PA–11726
p. 151: National Archives of Canada PA–142647
p. 165: National Archives of Canada PA–116450
p. 177: National Archives of Canada PA–152412
p. 189: Peter Bregg / *Maclean's*
p. 205: Peter Bregg / *Maclean's*
p. 214: Peter Bregg / *Maclean's*

http://www.harpercanada.com

HarperCollins books may be purchased for educational, business, or sales promotional use. For information please write: Special Markets Department, HarperCollins Canada, 55 Avenue Road, Suite 2900, Toronto, Ontario, Canada M5R 3L2.

First HarperCollins hardcover ed. IS BN 0-00-200027-X
First HarperCollins trade paper ed. IS BN 0-00-638563-X

Canadian Cataloguing in Publication Data

Granatstein, J. L., 1939–
Prime ministers: ranking Canada's leaders

"A Phyllis Bruce book".
ISBN 0-00-200027-X

1. Prime ministers — Canada.
I. Hillmer, Norman, 1942– . II. Title.

FC26.P7G72 1999   971'.009'9   C99-931159-X
F1005.G72 1999

99 00 01 02 03 04 HC 8 7 6 5 4 3
Printed and bound in the United States

Contents

Introduction

The race to the top of the political pole is a familiar image. Climbers vie with each other, struggling and manoeuvring, to reach the pinnacle. Once there, then what? Can they hold on, and what will they achieve as the inevitable slide downward begins? Some do well but most do not, and the measure of lasting achievement is not always obvious or clear.

Once prime ministers are in office, they must battle to stay there. There are always aspirants within their own ranks for the leadership—members of the Cabinet or the party caucus, or regional barons in provincial fiefdoms who want the job for themselves. Opposition parties wait for their chance in the next election and do mischief in the meantime. The media are anxious to build leaders up, but only as a prelude, it seems, to bringing them down. There is competition from the rulers who reside in our fantasies, who would be perfect if only some accident would catapult them to power. The dustbin of Canadian political history is littered with prime ministers who never were.

A coherent national vision is an important index of prime ministerial effectiveness, defining a leader's style and colouring public perception. Strong convictions and clear programs are an armour against doubts, of both the leader and the led, and give voters confidence there is substance and direction in their politics and politicians. Pierre Elliott Trudeau had an unshakeable view of a united Canada with a strong central government, while Brian Mulroney enunciated a clear free-trade policy in the 1988 election, setting a new course for the country and wiping some of his earlier miscues and miscalculations temporarily from memory. Mulroney believed that political capital had to be spent, not kept in the bank for some distant future. "If you're going to husband your political capital," he claimed, "you're going to get nothing done."

Yet decisiveness is not always its own reward, nor suited to a cautious and conservative people. A bold John A. Macdonald built the Canadian Pacific Railway in the nineteenth century. Trudeau confronted a terrorist crisis in Quebec head on in 1970. Joe Clark insisted on governing as if he had a majority of seats in the House of Commons in 1979, and brought in a controversial energy tax to boot. Mulroney initiated a process of constitutional accommodation in the Meech Lake and Charlottetown accords. How successful were they? Even though the road was bumpy and scandal-ridden, Macdonald's success in hatching the railway was the foundation of a glittering reputation. In each of the three modern cases, however, the architects of strong action were damaged badly, often at the time and always in historical memory.

Better to govern as Mackenzie King did, piling compromise on hesitation in this all too easily divided country? The height of his ambition, wrote the poet F.R. Scott after King's death,

> was to pile a Parliamentary Committee on a Royal Commission
> ... To let Parliament decide—

Introduction

Later.
Postpone, postpone, abstain.
. . . Truly he will be remembered
Wherever men honour ingenuity,
Ambiguity, inactivity, and political longevity.

King was said to understand Canadians so well because he was perfectly representative of the country, the repository of all our inadequacies and insecurities. For the *Globe and Mail* not so long ago, he was a man in Canada's image—unloved, timid, self-absorbed, opportunistic, puritanical, undistinguished, "governing always with the belief uppermost in his mind that Canadians would be constantly at one another's throats, culture against culture, region against region, faith against faith, if they were not continually coddled and conned into the illusion of brotherhood."

Character is vital, but it is intensely individual, and judgements about it are highly subjective. Mulroney's great failure was that he could not convince Canadians of his probity and sincerity. For now, that is what is remembered, not the series of strong initiatives of an activist prime minister. "Uncle Louis" St. Laurent became an icon of integrity and honesty, not to mention neighbourliness. "Mr. St. Laurent's great assets, which have helped him to win his huge majorities," *Saturday Night* stated near the end of his tenure, "have been his high character, his assiduous devotion to his duties, and his friendly ways." The magazine added that he had achieved the status of Grand Old Man, like John A. Macdonald and Wilfrid Laurier before him.

There is no substitute for good luck. Leaders get too much credit for prosperity, for example, and too much blame when the economy turns rancid. Laurier and St. Laurent governed in boom times. R.B. Bennett had to govern during the worst years of the Depression. King was fortunate to lose the election of 1930; he could return the next time stronger than ever, with his greatest moments ahead. Jean Chrétien had a better economy to work with than Mulroney did, and that is a major part of the reason why the Liberals of the 1990s were able to retain their popularity.

Crises test mettle and make reputations—or break them. Canada's wartime leaders faced dangers unknown to those who governed in relatively placid times. Sir Robert Borden pledged total victory in the First World War, cooperating with his British allies but also forcing them to acknowledge Canadian individuality and sacrifice. But he subordinated even the country's unity to the war effort. His ruthless imposition of conscription—compulsory military service—sorely divided Canada and wounded his party's Quebec hopes for years to come.

Learning from Borden, King offered a better balance between national and international obligations. "Not necessarily conscription, but conscription if necessary," he promised, in what became a memorable statement of purposeful ambiguity. The draft for service overseas was eventually implemented without the splits or political damage that Borden had suffered. Historians credit Borden with winning Canada's war, but criticize him for failing the test of national unity; they give King high grades for his ability to keep the country together during wartime, even if his methods and his style were unedifying.

Walter Lippmann, the great American journalist, contended that the goal and test of leadership is to inspire in others the will and conviction to carry on—no matter what. By this standard, Canadian prime ministers have for the most part been pale creatures, emphasizing the difficulties rather than the possibilities of their role. Canada was a hard country to

4

master, John A. moaned, and his successors repeated the complaint. Lester B. Pearson, speaking in 1965, elevated Canada to "the most difficult country in the world to govern." After two years of power, the former international diplomat joked, "I am perhaps a little more aware of that than I used to be."

Canada is not the most difficult country in the world to govern—China or India comes more readily to mind—but there are special challenges. The land is so vast, the population so thin. The disparities in wealth between individuals and regions are great, and the linguistic, religious, and class differences are sharp—and growing sharper. Canada's formative years were spent as a firmly rooted appendage of the British Empire, causing fierce loyalties and severe divisions. Colonialism stalks the land to this day: the United States, friendly though it is, diminishes Canadian identity and draws the young and talented like a magnet. The dialogue with the electorate, furthermore, has to take place in two official languages. Canadian political parties historically have been omnibus coalitions specializing in listening, understanding, and balancing interests, making room for everyone aboard and doling out a share of the spoils for all who come along for the ride. Political commentator Richard Gwyn has argued that Canada is not so much difficult to govern as it is hard to lead.

Once entrenched and even if uninspired, prime ministers are difficult to remove. Excluding those heads of government who served a few months, the average hold on power in Canada has been eight years. Four leaders—Macdonald, Laurier, King, and Trudeau—remained in office for fifteen years or more. Of those prime ministers elected in their own right, only Alexander Mackenzie and R.B. Bennett failed to win re-election at least once. Macdonald controlled the

Conservative Party between 1867 and 1891, and was prime minister for all but five years of that period.

Between them, Laurier and King led the Liberal Party from 1887 until 1948. Laurier was prime minister for fifteen years, King for twenty-two. Macdonald won four of the five campaigns he contested as the country's head, getting quick revenge for his only major defeat. Laurier, King, and Trudeau triumphed in three of four elections as prime minister, John Diefenbaker in two of three. If short-lived chiefs who never secured a real foothold are removed from the mix, only three prime ministers—Trudeau, Mulroney, and Chrétien—have ruled Canada since 1968. The last two won consecutive majority governments.

The trick in politics is to survive. Without that, there can be nothing, no argument the people are on side, no scope for action, and no lasting impression. The energetic John Thompson, the second of Macdonald's successors, had great potential, but a fatal heart attack eliminated him two years into his term. Charles Tupper, a doughty old fighter, came to office in 1896, late in his career and very late in the Conservative mandate. He was defeated after two months in the position, receiving more of the popular votes although many fewer of the seats. Arthur Meighen had two brief glimpses of the premiership in the 1920s, but he was unable to rein in his combative personality. An observer of the time said Meighen was a dogged and intelligent champion for the facts as he saw them, but an innocent to the Canadian style of politics. He insisted on playing the game by his rules, and he was always outclassed by his rival, Mackenzie King, not in intellect but in guile.

King was the master survivor of Canadian politics. He was personally unappetizing, without the charm and warmth of Macdonald or Laurier: one woman said that, after spending time with him, she felt as if she had been licked all over by a cat and had to rush to take a bath. What King did have, however, was a splendid sense of himself and his country. He understood the strengths and weaknesses of both. As his biographer Blair Neatby points out, he thought mass national popularity in a big and diverse country unlikely. He was content to remain in the background, the grey and solid man he knew he was. Unafraid to have strong ministers who could speak for their regions, he gave them prominence and listened carefully to their views. When there was criticism from Liberals, he absorbed it rather than suppressed it, recognizing that the party was the country writ small and could be a major force for national unity.

A prime minister's timing is critical—when to call an election, when to dismiss a minister, when to retire. Leaders who have known major success are apt to hang on too long, believing that the magic will happen again. Macdonald fought one campaign too many, dying shortly after the 1891 election without an adequately prepared successor. His party staggered into a long dark night of opposition. Trudeau and Mulroney clutched power late into their last terms and left their successors scant opportunity to make their marks.

Often leaders are defined by their contemporaries, for better or for worse. King had a series of opponents who were their own worst enemies. In contrast, the bitterly partisan Diefenbaker was able to drag Pearson into his swamp. Those who succeed powerful leaders are confounded by comparisons with their predecessor. Clark, taking over from Trudeau in 1979, inevitably looked like half a man. Trudeau, political writer Ron Graham saw, "was what Canadians wished to be—suave, intellectual, worldly, independent, and spontaneous. Clark was what Canadians feared they were—earnest, nice, honest, predictable, and rather dull . . . Canadians reacted against this fumbly, pompous reflection of themselves.

Joe Clark just wasn't good enough to make them greater." In a classic political cartoon, Trudeau swept back into the prime ministerial residence at 24 Sussex Drive after only nine months away, passing Clark at the door and instructing a minion to "Pay the Babysitter."

It can work the other way, too. Jean Chrétien, coming in the wake of Brian Mulroney, had only to be less glib and Gucci'd than the Tory. Even when he adopted Conservative policies on the Goods and Services Tax or North American free trade, his image remained positive, so well did he play up the stylistic contrasts.

Prime ministers must manage their Cabinets and parliamentary parties as well as the country. Cabinet formation is an art, sending the message that regional, racial, and religious interests will be respected and political favour distributed fairly. Previous loyalties and present abilities must be given their due, but sometimes a drone from Prince Edward Island, the only MP from the province, has to be given a harmless portfolio. Or southwestern Ontario, with a parcel of good members, can have only one place or two. Or there must be a Franco-Ontarian or a farmer to achieve the broadest possible representation.

The party caucus is another mystery, requiring exhortation, soothing, a nod of respect. Mulroney, a charmer close up, was a master of the technique. Liberal MPs under Chrétien could see their leader within forty-eight hours of asking, and he called the weekly gathering of members the "most important part of my week." Ministers were expected to be there and to take note. But what of dissent? "He is always very courteous in caucus," one of his MPs stated bluntly, "but it is very clear to all of us that it would be a really terrible idea if we displeased him." Bennett deployed considerable resources in organizing the caucus into a weapon of war in opposition, but once in power he paid it little attention, with disastrous results. He had to deal with knives in the back as well as spears from the front.

Strong prime ministers have preferred to keep their foes inside the tent. Mackenzie King, a fine delegator, made Saskatchewan powerhouse Charles Dunning one of his key ministers. Mulroney had Clark, the leader he had dethroned, as his foreign minister and later as his constitutional negotiator. Chrétien named Paul Martin, the man he had bested for the leadership, as finance minister for a critical period of deficit fighting. Fine leaders make this work, persuading their party foes that their time will come, that Canada needs them.

The weak and the unforgiving never learn to trust their adversaries. Diefenbaker brought the temple down on the party and on himself. Bennett could never forgive his trade minister, H.H. Stevens, for his independent stand on the country's economic woes, even when it would have been in the prime minister's interest to do so. "Ignorance can be forgiven," Bennett ranted, "stubbornness one understands, but treachery can neither be forgotten nor forgiven." In his fine biography of Canadian prime ministers, Michael Bliss points out that the great John A. Macdonald knew that public persons could not afford to harbour private resentments.

Our subject, then, is leadership failed and triumphant. The book began as a study carried out for *Maclean's*, appearing in the April 21, 1997, issue of that magazine. We based our findings on a canvass of twenty-six academics, a group of historians and political scientists (including ourselves) who were asked to rate the twenty prime ministers on a ten-point scale ranging from greatness at the high end to abject failure at the other. Each scholar was asked to write a commentary, justifying his or her rating. The results were averaged to form a ranked list, which we reported in *Maclean's* and use here as the basis of our analysis:

Prime Ministers

Great
1 William Lyon Mackenzie King
2 Sir John A. Macdonald
3 Sir Wilfrid Laurier

Near Great
4 Louis St. Laurent

High Average
5 Pierre Elliott Trudeau
6 Lester B. Pearson
7 Sir Robert Borden

Average
8 Brian Mulroney
9 Jean Chrétien
10 Sir John S. Thompson
11 Sir Alexander Mackenzie
12 R.B. Bennett
13 John Diefenbaker

Low Average
14 Arthur Meighen
15 Joe Clark

Failure
16 Sir Charles Tupper
17 Sir John J.C. Abbott
18 John Turner
19 Sir Mackenzie Bowell
20 Kim Campbell

Introduction

Those who participated in this study were Serge Bernier (National Defence Headquarters, Ottawa); Réal Bélanger (Université Laval); David J. Bercuson (University of Calgary); Michael Bliss (University of Toronto); Robert Bothwell (University of Toronto); Patrick Brennan (University of Calgary); Robert Craig Brown (University of Toronto); Penny Bryden (Mount Allison University); Margaret Conrad (Mount Saint Vincent University); René Durocher (Université de Montréal); Gerald Friesen (University of Manitoba); Jeffrey Keshen (University of Ottawa); Francine McKenzie (University of Toronto); Jacques Monet (Université de Sudbury); Desmond Morton (McGill University); John A. Munro (Vancouver); Peter F. Neary (University of Western Ontario); H. Blair Neatby (Carleton University); Patricia Roy (University of Victoria); Angelika Sauer (University of Winnipeg); David Smith (University of Saskatchewan); Denis Stairs (Dalhousie University); John Herd Thompson (Duke University); and Peter B. Waite (Dalhousie University).

These panelists, all eminent practitioners of their trade, were drawn from as broad a spectrum as we could devise. The judgements of senior and younger scholars were remarkably similar, as were those of women and men. French Quebecers valued the same qualities as did academics from the West or Atlantic Canada. All looked for prime ministers who could get, use, and keep power, who possessed clear goals and a strong sense of the country, who had the ability to knit consensus together and keep Canadians united, and who left behind a solid record of achievement.

Participants repeatedly warned about the dangers of the exercise. Political scientist David Smith spoke of the problem of "reverse perspective: characters growing larger the farther one is from them." He also claimed that prime ministers had little in common. "Rather than being a set of equals, they are actually unequal and therefore comparisons are probably invidious." Historian Blair Neatby countered that "we are not comparing apples and oranges. They were all leaders of political parties and that has meant achieving party unity in the face of strong regional loyalties. They were all trying to govern a country notable for the tensions thrown up by a precarious national sentiment, a powerful and not always sympathetic neighbour and cultural duality."

Francine McKenzie recommended that the leaders who had a chance to govern for only a few short months be called "ancillary prime ministers" and left unjudged or given a special category of their own. Since it takes many years before greatness or failure is apparent, there were also concerns about rating more recent leaders such as Mulroney and Chrétien. Campbell was put twentieth on the list, below even the egregious Mackenzie Bowell, the only prime minister to be removed from office by a revolt of his Cabinet. How else to explain Campbell's last-place ranking, except by fresh memories and dashed expectations?

Today's scoundrel can be tomorrow's hero, depending on how events and perceptions alter interpretations. In 1948, when he retired, few would have guessed that Mackenzie King would rank first on a list of prime ministers forty years later. Mulroney does not currently stand high in the eyes of his people, but ten or twenty years on perceptions may have shifted, putting him higher or lower than he is placed here. In an interview with the Ottawa *Citizen* half a decade after leaving office, Mulroney understood this well. "Five years is nothing in terms of history. The main question will be, 'Did your initiatives survive the test of time?' It'll all come out in the fullness of time—good, bad or indifferent."

Introduction

The first of our many obligations is to the members of the academic panel, who provided us with their frank assessments of the prime ministers. The accounts that follow in this book, however, are ours alone, the product of personal hopes and biases.

Phyllis Bruce is a publisher and editor *sans pareil*. Rosemary Shipton questioned our judgements and encouraged us to write more forcefully. Boris Stipernitz helped collect the book's photographs and cartoons, and *Maclean's* generously provided us with some from the magazine's archive. Charlotte Gray read a number of the chapters, sharpening the prose and providing us with research materials. Roger Sarty improved the Laurier section immeasurably. Stephen Azzi, Grant Dawson, David Farr, William Kaplan, Hector Mackenzie, and Blair Neatby all gave good advice, some of which we followed. Elaine Granatstein and Anne Hillmer have our love and gratitude, as ever.

Sir John A. Macdonald

The Grand Old Man, they called him, and Sir John A. Macdonald set the master pattern for Canadian prime ministers. Balancing differences of region, religion, class, and profession, Macdonald understood instinctively how to govern an intractable nation. By force of will and strength of national vision, he made it work, and, for a time, Canadians forgot what a skilful trickmaster it took to lead them.

Born in Glasgow, Scotland, January 11, 1815; died in Ottawa, June 6, 1891. Prime minister for nineteen years: July 1, 1867–November 5, 1873; October 17, 1878–June 6, 1891

In the election of March 1891 the crowds had turned out to hear the prime minister as he campaigned victoriously once more for his party. They had cheered him to the echo, and one leather-lunged enthusiast yelled out, "You'll never die, John A." But in the early days of June he lay desperately ill from a massive stroke in his second-floor bedroom at Earnscliffe, his splendid home between the Ottawa River and Sussex Drive. The city council, concerned for the dying prime minister's comfort, directed that trams on Sussex be forbidden from clanging their bells. It was to no avail, and Sir John succumbed on June 6. The story, probably apocryphal, has it that the bylaw was never repealed and, although trams no longer run on Sussex, no bells remains the rule.

At the age of five, Macdonald came from Glasgow to Kingston, Upper Canada, where his father tried, with little success, to make his fortune. The family gave the boy a good education—good enough that, when he was fifteen, he began to article in the office of a Kingston lawyer. Five years later he opened his own law firm and quickly became known for his willingness to take on hard cases and provide a spirited, ingenious defence. At the same time, he invested in businesses, speculated in property, and became a director of companies. Macdonald was a natural for politics.

After some years in local politics, Macdonald won election to the legislature of the Canadas in 1844. Still struggling to achieve responsible government, Upper and Lower Canada

Sir John A. Macdonald

National Archives of Canada C–21604

Sir John at the height of his powers.

were rough societies, divided by language and religion.

Macdonald's views were initially conventional: attachment to Britain and Queen Victoria, and belief in the economic development of the country. Demonstrating a pragmatic willingness to do what was necessary to serve his and his electors' interests, he rose fairly rapidly and played major roles in the governments formed by the emerging alliance of Upper Canadian conservatives and Lower Canadian *bleus*. By 1856 he was the Upper Canadian leader. He resisted the democratic "rep by pop" arguments of the Upper Canadian Clear Grits (Reformers, later to be called

Liberals) and supported cautious, slow change rather than a wholesale shift of power to wherever the majority lived. In 1864, when George Brown, the Grit leader and publisher of Toronto's *Globe* newspaper, urged that a coalition be formed to bring about constitutional change in the Canadas, Macdonald was in his element—particularly after the idea expanded to include the confederation of the British North American colonies. In a negotiation as complicated as this one, his pragmatism was essential, his oratory galvanized voters and colonial negotiators alike, and his fear of the United States, then tearing itself apart in the Civil War, created genuine urgency out of what might have been desultory discussions.

Confederation in 1867 was not Macdonald's sole creation. Politicians such as Brown, George Étienne Cartier, and Charles Tupper played enormous roles, and the British government had the ultimate responsibility in a constitutional sense. Still, it is safe to say that, without Macdonald's flexibility, dynamism, and sense of vision, the union of the Canadas, New Brunswick, and Nova Scotia into the Dominion of Canada could not have occurred. The British North America Act, in effect, the Canadian Constitution, was largely his handiwork, and he is said to have drafted fifty of the clauses in the bill. He was the only colonial leader to be knighted, and, inevitably, he was the politician asked by the governor general to lead the first government of the new nation.

Macdonald's tasks as prime minister were overwhelming. He had to create an administration for the new federal government, from establishing a militia to setting up the postal system and staffing the various departments of government. He had to weld the disaffected into supporting the new country. He had to shape a national political party out of politicians affected with extreme cases of "localitis," and in many cases bitterly opposed to or mistrustful of one another. Still others, stubbornly opposed to Confederation, had to be fought even after the British North America Act was drafted and, like the Nova Scotian Joseph Howe, carefully seduced into joining the national government. Macdonald was helped in his task by his tolerance. "I never asked the question, and never will ask, what a man's religion, race or ancestry may be," he proclaimed. "If he is a capable man, 'the right man for the right place,' that is all I inquire into."

Above all, Macdonald had to give a sense of purpose and continuity to the nation by expanding both east and west. He wanted Prince Edward Island and Newfoundland to join Confederation, but he succeeded only in bringing in the smaller island. He hoped to secure British Columbia as well, and did so by promising to construct a railway to the Pacific Coast—a costly, high-risk venture through unmapped wilderness and unexplored mountains. Then, in 1870, he had to put down a rebellion at the Red River settlement led by a young and charismatic Métis named Louis Riel. In the aftermath of the rebellion, Manitoba became a province, but the West, with all its rich resources and lands, was still not secure. The British troops that had been instumental in defeating the rebels were withdrawn from Canada that same year, and Macdonald had now to keep the United States at bay. Many of the most powerful American leaders remained convinced that their nation's Manifest Destiny was to control all of North America.

These tasks were beyond the capacity of any one man. The Americans could be negotiated with, though, in the years before Canada had its own diplomats, it required patience and guile to deal with the scheming Uncle Sam through British negotiators who were more willing to give in to Washington than to satisfy Ottawa's needs. At home, Macdonald

"WE IN CANADA SEEM TO HAVE LOST ALL IDEA OF JUSTICE, HONOR AND INTEGRITY."—THE MAIL, 26TH SEPTEMBER.

The Pacific Scandal delighted cartoonists of the day.

used patronage with great skill to tie the country together. A postmastership in New Glasgow could make a loyal Canadian out of a Nova Scotian provincialist; a wharf in Victoria could make a nationalist out of a Vancouver Islander. If these voters supported John A.'s party, all the better. He won the first two elections held in the new dominion, and each victory solidified the nation, the Conservative Party, and his own power. Aware of his abilities, but not vain, Macdonald understood the importance of power. He had things to do and he was confident that he alone could do them.

In the 1872 election, Macdonald and his Quebec lieutenant, Cartier, solicited donations from rich men who were seeking the contracts to build the railway to the Pacific. In all, more than $350,000—a huge sum in 1870s dollars—went to support Conservative candidates. Inevitably, this story of the Pacific Scandal leaked out, and the "loose fish" in John A's party began to swim to safety with the opposition. Some members of parliament were Tories so long as John A. was in good shape and patronage could flow their way. Once he was in difficulty, they would desert in a flash. The majority from the 1872 election disappeared in the House of Commons, and by the time Macdonald was forced to resign in late 1873, he was in a gin-induced haze. The Liberals under the upright stonemason Alexander Mackenzie took office and won a sweeping victory at the beginning of 1874, campaigning against the corruption of Macdonald and his men.

John A. was no stranger to adversity. His first wife died only fourteen years into their marriage, and one of their two children died in childhood. The daughter from his second marriage was hydrocephalic. These personal troubles were tragic, and he drowned his sorrows too often. The political disaster of the Pacific Scandal plunged him into deep despair and alcoholism.

Gradually, he worked his way back to sobriety and into the good graces of the nation. The Liberals helped, stumbling repeatedly as they tried to find a way to move the railway, which almost everyone agreed was essential, along at the lowest possible cost and the slowest possible speed. They could be criticized for their lack of faith in Canada, and Macdonald was scathing in his denunciations. But he needed something more, a policy that could help voters forget the Pacific Scandal. By 1877 Macdonald hit upon the winning policy—a tariff on US imports that offered protection for infant Canadian industries and, simultaneously, generated revenues for government use. The Tories were soon hailing their "National Policy." With the country mired in a period of growing economic uncertainty, the promise of high tariffs did the trick. In the general election of 1878 the voters, ready to forget if not yet forgive, swept John A. back into office. Opportunism and political chicanery—or so the defeated Alexander Mackenzie moaned—had triumphed over honest government.

Now in his sixties, Macdonald was unquestionably a superb politician. The caricaturists loved him, finding his craggy face and large nose a superb subject. The story was told of a member of parliament entering the parliamentary barbershop to see the barber holding the prime minister's nose as he shaved his upper lip. "I suppose, Sir John, that he is the only man in Canada who can take you by the nose with impunity?" the MP asked. "Yes," John A. replied, "and he has his hands full."

Macdonald always appeared agreeable, promising something to everyone and delivering often enough to keep his supporters in line. He preferred a honeyed phrase to harsh words, and he could pile flattery on top of praise as well as any man. Canada was a hard enough country to govern: Why alienate people unnecessarily? His talents were especially necessary with French Canada, a Quebec always suspicious that its *amour propre* and its interests were likely to be neglected by Anglo politicians. Not by Macdonald. He used appointments judiciously and dealt with the province through his lieutenants, first Cartier and then Hector Langevin, to make sure that the politicians, the church, and the people were kept on side. Above all, he was always a pragmatist. To help himself remain on top, he could adjust the electoral boundaries to produce the desired outcome. After the 1881 Census, Ontario was completely reconfigured, enough to deliver fifty-five of the province's seats in the 1882 election to John A.'s Tories.

Macdonald understood that a government, if it wanted to remain in office, could not always operate on its principles. "There are often times," he said once, "when I do things that are against my conscience, and which I know are wrong; but if I do not make certain allowances for the weakness of human nature, my party would turn me out of power, and those who took my place would manage things worse than I." Consistency had its virtues, but flexibility had more. His vision was long, and he was ready to make detours along the way if the goal remained in sight.

Sometimes, however, hard and divisive choices had to be made; other times, the demands of the majority of Canadians had to be heard, no matter what Quebec thought. In 1884 rumours of unrest in the North-West Territories (now Saskatchewan and Alberta) began to reach Ottawa, as settlers felt their needs had been continually overlooked by a far-away federal government. The Indian tribes were similarly unhappy and so, too, were the Métis, who had been forced to move farther west after the 1870 Red River Rebellion. All that was needed to set the Prairies alight was a leader. When Louis Riel, charismatic, well educated in a Quebec seminary, but by 1884 almost certainly mad, returned to Canada from his exile in the United States, Ottawa felt it had no choice but to get involved. There were no British troops to do the job this time. The Militia, the country's enthusiastic but ill-trained and ill-equipped citizen soldiery, rode the Canadian Pacific Railway as far as it went, then marched the rest of the way. After several sharp skirmishes, some lost but most won more by good luck than good generalship, the soldiers had put down the second Riel Rebellion. Taken prisoner, Riel was tried, found guilty, and sentenced to death for treason.

Quebec had generally supported the nation's military response to the revolt, and francophone militia had participated in the campaign. To hang Riel was a different matter, and the Quebec politicians and press demanded clemency. After all, was Riel not delusionary? Likely he was, but to Macdonald, the law must take its course. Unwisely, he once said that Riel would swing though every dog in Quebec bark in his favour. More coolly, he wrote a confrere: "I felt it would have been an act of political insanity to yield" to the clamour "simply because the man was of French blood." Riel went to the gallows, and the only good that came from the unhappy affair was the more rapid completion of the railway to the Pacific. In the 1887 election, fought over the corpse of Riel, John A. lost seats in Quebec, but still won easily.

The Riel Rebellion and its aftermath had a major impact on the country. The easy tolerance that had always been Macdonald's personal style had suddenly gone out of fashion at much the same time that "nativist" sentiment was sweeping through the United States. In Canada, Protestants mistrusted Catholics, and French Canadians feared their English-speaking compatriots. Though always in the majority, Protestant Ontarians suddenly began to feel that they were under siege. When the government of Quebec settled a long-standing claim by the Jesuit Order over religious property that had been seized after the Conquest of New France, the issue exploded. Equal rights, the cry went up: the Pope shall not rule in Canada! It was farcical, but it was serious, and the Conservative Party fragmented as Protestant extremists, hitherto tame back-benchers, began to look at Macdonald as all too accommodating to the "damn Frenchies." Moreover, hadn't Macdonald made John Thompson, a Protestant-born Nova Scotian who had converted to Roman Catholicism, his minister of justice? Were the ancient rights of British Canadians to be sacrificed to the whims of Rome and Jesuitical French Canadians?

In this climate, the Manitoba Schools Question dominated the political landscape. In Winnipeg the provincial government had come out for "national schools," schools that would treat all—Protestant and Catholic, French and English—equally. But francophones in the province believed that their language was an essential part of their children's education, and Catholics thought that their separate schools had been guaranteed. Macdonald wanted the courts to settle the question, not the Parliament of Canada, and he was wise to stall. His successors had to face the issue.

As Macdonald entered the 1890s, the other troubling issue of the day was the nation's lack of prosperity. Somehow, despite the potential of the land, the times remained hard. Immigrants came from Britain and Europe, but tens of thousands left each year for the greener pastures of the United States, and the population grew very slowly. The National Policy had the support of manufacturers, but farmers hated the high costs it forced on them, and workers resented paying more for imported goods—even if their jobs depended on the tariff wall. Perhaps, Macdonald thought, some way could be found to strike a trade arrangement with the United States, exactly as the Liberals, now led by Wilfrid Laurier, had been saying and as Alexander Mackenzie had tried vainly to secure in his time in office. Secret discussions with Washington went nowhere, to Macdonald's regret, and when the election came in 1891, the Liberals were all out for reciprocity, as free trade was called. Unrestricted reciprocity, Laurier said, was the key to prosperity.

Macdonald was equal to the challenge and ready to turn his party policy on a dime. Free trade was all but treason, he thundered now, the selling out of Canada's proud British

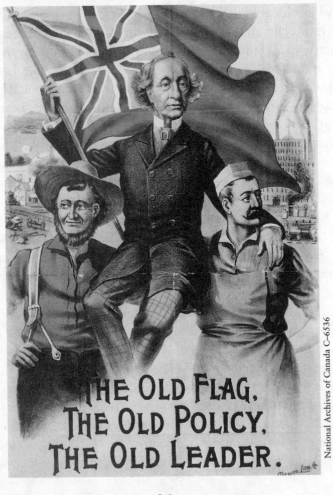

THE OLD FLAG,
THE OLD POLICY,
THE OLD LEADER.

National Archives of Canada C-6536

heritage for a mess of American stew. The Liberals wanted to see Canada annexed to the United States. Not him. "I am a British subject and British born," he said in a major speech on February 17, "and a British subject I hope to die." It was more than a little unscrupulous, but it was enormously successful as the Tories campaigned for "the old flag, the old party, the old policy." Laurier was outmanoeuvred and went down to defeat, he and his party branded as traitors.

It was Sir John's last hurrah. He died three months after the election in his seventy-seventh year.

Without question, Macdonald was one of the nation's greatest leaders. He had made Confederation run. He devised the style of national leadership, recognizing that, to succeed in Canada, a government and a party had to have English and French representation, and a Cabinet had to comprise representatives of provinces and regions, Protestants and Catholics, farmers and city folk. He understood that sugar caught more flies than vinegar, that patronage was necessary in a society where jobs were scarce, and that new loyalties had to be created before they could be welded together into a Canadian nationalism. There was no doubt of his own nationalism. He said once, "Since I was five years old, I have been in Canada. My affections, my family are here. All my hopes and remembrances are Canadian; and not only are my principles and prejudices Canadian, but . . . my interests are Canadian."

He could certainly make the tough decisions, but he much preferred to delay, delay, and delay again rather than divide the nation unnecessarily or disappoint a region or an individual. "Old Tomorrow," some called Macdonald. He also had endless charm, and he used it knowingly to bind men to him. He understood that loyalty to the leader was an important factor in governing successfully. There were few political devices he would not employ, few shameless bargains he would hesitate to make. Perhaps he drank too much and too often to deal with despair, both personal and political. Yet Canadians looked at the Grand Old Man and decided they preferred Macdonald drunk to anyone else of his era sober. He was a leader of genius when Canada needed one.

You'll never die, John A., they had shouted in 1891, and it was true.

Sir Alexander Mackenzie

A Scots stonemason by trade, Mackenzie was as solid a man as could be found. Honest, incorruptible, unbending, a man who created great national institutions, he stood in stark contrast with the easier, pliable John A. Macdonald. There was no foresight or flexibility, however, and eventually the voters fled Mackenzie for the devil they knew—and liked.

Born in Logierait, Scotland, January 28, 1822; died in Toronto, April 17, 1892. Prime minister for five years: November 7, 1873–October 9, 1878

Had he immigrated to Upper Canada a few years earlier than he did, Alexander Mackenzie would certainly have lined up behind his fellow Scot, William Lyon Mackenzie, during the Upper Canadian rebellion of 1837. His scorn for privilege, his dislike of the established position of the Church of England, his distaste for the pretensions of the elites and the upper classes almost guaranteed that he might have been driven into exile with the "little rebel" or, worse still, executed. Fate instead brought Mackenzie to Canada in 1842, five years after the rebellions.

His origins were among the Scottish working poor. His family was large, the income small, the scrambling for wages never-ending. He had begun working full time when he was thirteen, he was an apprentice stonemason three years later, and a journeyman stone cutter at twenty. There was no chance to get ahead in Scotland, but there might be in North America, so in 1842 he went to the Canadas. He found work in Kingston, helping to construct the Martello towers that were designed to fend off the Yankees.

After he followed his brother to Port Sarnia in 1846, he became a contractor, erecting houses and public buildings throughout southwestern Upper Canada and building a repu-tation for quality and efficiency. Though he was prospering, he maintained his egalitarianism and, by 1851, was well known in Clear Grit circles, a prominent Reformer in his part of the country. The next year he became editor of the local

THE MODERN NERO.

FIDDLING AT THE DESTRUCTION OF CANADIAN COMMERCE.

Bengough / National Archives of Canada C-78781

Hard times would severely challenge Mackenzie.

newspaper, but he did not make the jump into electoral politics until his brother, who had won a seat in an 1860 by-election, had decided politics was no life for him. In 1861 Alexander Mackenzie was elected to stand at the side of George Brown, the publisher of the *Globe* and the leader of the Clear Grits. Mackenzie supported the drive for Confederation, but he was much less enthusiastic when Brown joined in the Great Coalition of 1864 that preceded it, largely because he feared that, in any coalition party, principles had to be sacrificed. That was typical of Mackenzie: principles mattered to him—indeed, they were life itself.

REHEARSING FOR THE 23RD INSTANT.

M—K—ZIE—"I WILL FIGHT HIM UPON THIS THEME UNTIL MY EYELIDS WILL NO LONGER WAG!"—HAMLET, ACT V., SCENE 1.　　JOHN A.—"WHAT DO I FEAR?"—RICHARD III., ACT V., SCENE 3.

The Pacific Scandal gave Mackenzie his chance to govern.

As one of the group of leading opposition Liberals, as they now called themselves, Mackenzie worked in harness with a team of some talent, including Edward Blake, a great orator and one-time premier of Ontario. They had no designated leader, a state of affairs that condemned them to perpetual opposition. In 1872 Macdonald won another term, and, finally in the fall of 1873, the federal Liberals recognized reality and chose Mackenzie as their chief.

Sir Alexander Mackenzie

Macdonald's government quickly fell apart over the Pacific Scandal. The Tories had seen nothing wrong in accepting huge sums of money to fight the 1872 election from speculators interested in the charter to build the railway to the West. The public disagreed, and Macdonald was forced to resign. In November 1873, without benefit of an election, Mackenzie became prime minister and, shrewdly, called a quick election in January 1874. Canadians swept the Liberals back into office, and it seemed that Macdonald was so discredited by corruption that the Liberals had a generation in office ahead of them.

And so it might have been if only Mackenzie had been able to compromise; if the prime minister had been able to chivvy his colleagues along; if he and the Liberals had just a touch of Macdonald's vision for the future; or if his speeches in the raucous House of Commons could have inspired the country. But Mackenzie suffered for his dour, stubborn approach to life. Many of his colleagues looked not to him but to the brilliant Blake as their natural chief. Blake thought so too, but he was mercurial, difficult, and flighty. Although he sat briefly in the Mackenzie Cabinet, he resigned a month after the victorious election of January 1874. The lost leader thereafter sniped at the prime minister, joining others Mackenzie had counted on. Many of the best Grits chose to remain outside the Cabinet, and their lack of trust hurt and puzzled Mackenzie. Why would they not support him?

Still, Mackenzie did his stonemason's level best. An honest man in an era of open corruption, he cherished the idea of a secret ballot and elections in all ridings on the same day, and he implemented these efforts to prevent corrupt practices for future federal elections. He established the Supreme Court of Canada. Convinced that Canada needed to develop its own well-educated army officers, he created the Royal Military

College in Kingston. These were lasting achievements, but they scarcely touched the main issue of the day.

That issue was railways. Macdonald's government had been corrupt, but it knew that a transcontinental rail line was essential to bind Canada together with a road of steel. Mackenzie too wanted a railway, but where the Tories had been prepared to risk federal moneys to get it built as quickly as possible, Mackenzie was far too cautious for that. Government funding meant tax increases, and that could never be popular in a difficult, depressed economy. Moreover, whom would the railway serve? The Prairies were nearly empty of homesteaders, populated only by the native people, and there were but a handful of settlers behind the mountains in British Columbia. Yet the Pacific colony had entered Confederation on the promise of the railway to link it to central Canada. The result of all the conflicting pressures was that Mackenzie moved slowly ahead with surveys, planning, and preliminaries—12,000 miles surveyed and the construction of a telegraph line from Port Arthur to Edmonton—but with not as much progress as British Columbians or Canadians wanted. His concern for public funds was commendable, but the want of vision was not. Mackenzie's record here has to be counted a failure.

Another of Mackenzie's aims was to secure a free trade agreement with the United States to replace the 1854 treaty the Yanks had cancelled at the end of the Civil War. He made his old leader, George Brown, the chief negotiator of the British team in 1874, Canada not yet having the right to handle its own diplomatic relations. Brown tried hard and actually achieved an agreement that was sweeping in its terms, but in the end Mackenzie and the Liberal government had no luck. The US Senate adjourned with the agreement unratified, and Canadian manufacturers and other special interest groups had seen enough to believe that the deal was bad for them. What made matters worse was that Mackenzie now had to raise tariffs to secure revenue—the tariff being the government's major source of funds in the era before income tax. A tariff for revenue was acceptable, he argued; a tariff for the protection of manufacturers was not. Few Canadians grasped the distinction; all tariffs raised the prices they paid for goods imported into Canada.

Macdonald saw instinctively that the tariff was a powerful political tool. To him, Canada needed a National Policy of tariff protection for infant industries, and he eagerly led his Tories into battle in the 1878 election. Mackenzie had waited until the last possible moment to call the vote, always a sign of weakness, and his party was less well organized than it should have been. A strong campaigner, with a sharp tongue and humour that was biting rather than laugh provoking, Mackenzie as always did his best. But Macdonald was in great form: the National Policy was a powerful weapon, and five years in opposition had blurred the memory of the Pacific Scandal. Mackenzie was doomed. His strong point was that he had been a stonemason, his political opponents joked, and his weak point was that he remained a stonemason. The Liberals went down to a crushing defeat, and Macdonald was back in the prize seat.

By 1880, the Liberals' demands for Mackenzie's resignation as leader were loud, and he gave way to Edward Blake. Although he remained a member of parliament, his days of power and prominence were ended. Mackenzie was a good and decent man, honourable and honest. He rose from modest beginnings to make a successful life. Was it his fault that he faced the charismatic Macdonald? Was he to blame that Canadians preferred the jocular deviousness of John A. to the rock-solid bluntness of Mackenzie? He was incorruptible in an age of widespread graft, he had a working man's concern for the way public funds should be spent, and he laid the foundation for some of Canada's great institutions. Those are no mean achievements, but today Mackenzie, all but completely forgotten, gets scant credit for any of them.

1
2
3
4
5
6
7
8
9
10
11
12
13
14
15
16
17
18
19
20

Sir John J.C. Abbott, Sir John S. Thompson, Sir Mackenzie Bowell, Sir Charles Tupper

(left to right)

Four prime ministers in five years—a record of futility and frustration, culminating in electoral defeat. The Tory successors to Sir John A. Macdonald remain almost unknown and unsung, a gaggle of sectarians and senators without popular appeal. Yet Sir John Thompson might, with luck and better health, have made a mark.

17 *Sir John J.C. Abbott, born in St. Andrew, Lower Canada, March 12, 1821; died in Montreal, October 30, 1893. Prime minister for one year: June 16, 1891–November 24, 1892*

10 *Sir John S. Thompson, born in Halifax, November 10, 1845; died in Windsor, England, December 12, 1894. Prime minister for two years: December 5, 1892–December 12, 1894*

19 *Sir Mackenzie Bowell, born in Rickinghall, England, December 27, 1823; died in Belleville, Ontario, December 10, 1917. Prime minister for one year: December 21, 1894–April 27, 1896*

16 *Sir Charles Tupper, born in Amherst, Nova Scotia, July 2, 1821; died in Bexley Heath, England, October 20, 1915. Prime minister for two months: May 1, 1896–July 8, 1896*

John A. left his country many legacies, not least Confederation, the National Policy, and a record of political success that resonates down the ages. But he was less kind to his party. Although he won his last election in 1891 to the cheers of his supporters and the country, the Grand Old Man died three months after his last victory. Confusion reigned in his wake.

Not that there wasn't a logical successor. Sir John Thompson, the Nova Scotian and minister of justice, was widely considered the ablest member of the Cabinet, a man of intelligence, probity, and substantial charm. But he suffered from

Sir John Thompson, third from left, at a family outing.

one drawback: born a Protestant, he had converted to Roman Catholicism when he married. In the heated sectarian climate of the day, when religion was a defining characteristic, this affiliation was enough to brand him a "pervert." It would not be Thompson—yet.

Instead, the choice fell on Sir John Abbott, a lawyer, McGill law dean, wealthy businessman, and senator. Abbott was the first to lead the government from the upper chamber. He had signed the annexation manifesto of 1849, calling on Canada to join the United States if Britain's policy of free trade turned against Canadian exports. He had made up for that youthful error by his work for the Canadian Pacific Railway, by his winning election after election to Parliament in Quebec, and by his service as minister of trade and commerce under Macdonald.

Abbott had not wanted the prime ministership, but Thompson's Roman Catholicism ruled him out; Sir Hector Langevin, long Macdonald's Quebec lieutenant, was enmeshed in a huge scandal in the Department of Public Works; and Sir Charles Tupper, the high commissioner in London, enjoyed his life abroad too much to return home. So Abbott, seventy years old and in failing health, got the nod, at least until those who objected to Thompson's religion calmed down.

Abbott led the Senate, and Thompson the House of Commons, and the arrangement appeared to work well. The Tories won a slew of by-elections and managed to deal with the Langevin scandal by dropping him from the Cabinet. But Abbott was not happy: "I hate politics," he wrote, "and what are considered their appropriate methods. I hate notoriety, public meetings, public speeches, caucuses, and everything that I know of that is apparently the necessary incident of politics—except doing public work to the best of my ability." He had some ability, too, but his health went rapidly downhill under the strain of office and the party managers tried desperately to boost support for Thompson. Sam Hughes, a spokesman for Ontario Orangemen and rabid anti-Catholics, was eventually persuaded to give his backing to the Nova Scotian, and he wrote to Thompson that "the boys" now wanted him: "What! The pervert? The ultramontane? The roman catholic? . . . Yes, all say yes."

In November 1892 Abbott gratefully stepped down. The new leader was young—only forty-seven—and he projected a dignified air with his slightly portly frame. Thompson was a lawyer, a devoted husband to his wife, Annie—their love letters testify to how close they remained throughout their marriage—and a good father to his five surviving children (four had died in infancy). Thompson had risen from the Nova Scotia legislature and, briefly, from the provincial premiership to the bench until, in 1885, Macdonald persuaded him to come to Ottawa as justice minister. "The great discovery of my life," Sir John A. said, "was my discovery of Thompson." He did well from the start, his polished oratory and quiet good sense and intelligence impressing everyone, not least in the way he handled the fierce debate in Parliament over the execution of Louis Riel during his first few months in office. He also had to stickhandle the government's response as angry Protestants tried to force the disallowance of Quebec's settlement of the Jesuits' Estates Question in 1889. This issue fed the flames of religious bigotry and led to denunciations of Thompson. The emergence of the Manitoba Schools Question at the beginning of the 1890s made religion the dominant political issue in the land.

Was Canada to be Protestant or Catholic? Were the schools to be public, which ordinarily meant Protestant, or religious, by which all meant Roman Catholic? Were francophones in the West to be allowed to attend school in their own language? Was Canada, above all, to be French or English? All these critical questions reverberated widely when the Manitoba government passed legislation creating a province-wide public or "national" school system. There must be remedial legislation, Catholics cried, demanding that Ottawa use its constitutional powers to remedy the ills that the elimination of their schools had forced upon them.

An issue like this one was a nightmare for any political party, and Conservatives and Liberals alike tried desperately to keep French and English, Protestant and Catholic working in harness in their ranks. The Manitoba question, of course, was worse still for Thompson, the converted Catholic. Indeed, Ontario Protestant MP Dalton McCarthy created the Equal Rights faction within the Tory Party during Thompson's tenure as justice minister and complained that the Protestant majority was being denied its proper place.

Using his judicious tact and strong hand, Prime Minister Thompson tried to damp down the flames of sectarianism with some success. He did not move quickly, as he probably ought to have done, to pass remedial legislation for Manitoba, instead referring the case to the courts. We can sympathize with the difficulties he must have faced at the thought of quick action to help Manitoba Catholics. Instead, to prove his openness to militant Protestantism, he brought Ontario Orangeman N. Clarke Wallace, one of the "noble thirteen" who had voted against the government on the question of the Jesuits' Estates settlement in Parliament, into the Cabinet.

Above all, Thompson concentrated on economic questions, reforming the tariff, creating the trade commissioner service abroad, and negotiating trade agreements. He was on the way to building a good record and possibly keeping Conservatism in power when, during a mission to Britain and the Continent, he went to visit Queen Victoria at Windsor Castle in December 1894. He had been feeling unwell, but the queen wanted to make him a member of the Imperial Privy Council, a high honour. At the lunch following the ceremony, he collapsed, and died at once.

The great "might-have-been" of Canadian prime ministers, Thompson left his widow and children with little money. The British government returned his body to Canada on a Royal Navy cruiser, and the ceremonies in Halifax were heartfelt. But with Thompson gone, the splits in the Tory Party were now revealed all too clearly.

Governor General Lord Aberdeen and his meddlesome

wife, Ishbel, could not abide Sir Charles Tupper—a Father of Confederation, long-time Cabinet minister, and Canadian representative in London—because of his record as a rake and suspicions that he was not quite honest. They simply would not have Tupper as their prime minister, the Aberdeens maintained. Astonishingly, they called on Sir Mackenzie Bowell, another senator, and the septuagenarian trade minister, to form a government.

Bowell was the owner of the Belleville *Daily Intelligencer* and a longtime politician, steeped in the rituals of the fiercely Protestant Orange Lodge, of which he had been Grand Master. He was not a skilled leader, and he proved completely inept at making decisions or managing his Cabinet and Parliament. His ministers— a "nest of traitors," he called them—treated him with contempt, and in January 1896 half the Cabinet resigned in protest at his leadership on the Manitoba Schools Question. Bowell had bobbed and weaved, trying to avoid the necessity of forcing remedial legislation through his Cabinet and the House of Commons. When he finally

National Archives of Canada PA–12359

Bowell, in Windsor uniform, looking much fiercer than he was.

had no option other than to act, he still managed to waste a year in acute indecision. When he did move, it was too late. In

April 1896 the inept prime minister was finally forced out of office by his ministers and his party.

This time, the Aberdeens had no choice but to accept Sir Charles Tupper. The new prime minister was seventy-six years old in 1896, but, unlike Abbott and Bowell, he retained the vigour that, in his youth, had led jealous husbands to label him the "Ram of the Cumberland." His party's position was far from enviable. The constitutionally mandated five-year life of the government was running out fast and an election had to be held. The Conservative Party was divided, factionalized, and near destroyed in its Ontario base by the tensions between Catholics and Protes-

Sir Charles Tupper

National Archives of Canada C–81239

tants. The Liberal opposition, led by the francophone Quebecer Wilfrid Laurier, was gaining ground daily, and Tupper had no time to reverse the trend against the government.

The old man was almost up to the challenge. A doctor, he had made a start in politics in Nova Scotia in the 1850s, supported Confederation in the 1860s, and was largely responsible for bringing the province into the union. He joined Macdonald's Cabinet in 1870 and served in senior portfolios until he went to Britain as high commissioner in 1883. With the exception of a brief period as Sir John A.'s finance minister in 1887–88, he held that post in London until Bowell's removal. Tupper reconstructed the Cabinet, finding some Quebec Catholics willing to believe his fervent pledge that he would press remedial legislation through the House if he could win the election. Then he dissolved Parliament and went to the electors. He campaigned vigorously across the land, making powerful speeches about the Manitoba Schools Question and the tariff, but to no avail. Laurier's calculated vagueness and promise of "sunny ways" as the method to resolve the wretched Manitoba question defeated Tupper and the Tories.

The Conservatives, in power continuously for eighteen years, had lost the talent for governing Canada. The political magician Macdonald had been able to keep all the balls in the air with great skill, and Thompson just possibly might have been able to do so. Abbott and Bowell were hopeless, though Tupper, given more opportunity, conceivably might have succeeded. But there was no more time.

Sir Wilfrid Laurier

He was the first French-Canadian prime minister, charming, imaginative, and gentle, an expert in the softness of compromise and the hard use of power. While making a place for his people in the Liberal Party and an autonomous niche for Canada within the British Empire, Wilfrid Laurier calmly presided over the expansion of the West and the great ferment of industrialization. In 1911 free trade with the United States seemed certain to prolong his hold on power, but fears of Yankee domination drove him from office.

Born in St.-Lin, Canada East, November 20, 1841; died in Ottawa, February 17, 1919. Prime minister for fifteen years: July 11, 1896–October 6, 1911

In 1897 Liberal prime minister Wilfrid Laurier travelled to England for the celebrations to mark the sixtieth anniversary of Victoria as queen of Britain and its huge empire, Canada included. Fifty-six years old, in public life for twenty years, he had never before crossed the Atlantic Ocean. He hated to travel, preferring to be as close as possible to his wife, Zoë, and the home he still maintained in the small Quebec town of Arthabaska.

With his shock of flowing hair, upright bearing, and stylish dress, Laurier was an impressive figure in the imperial capital. Fresh from having given the British a trade advantage in the Canadian market, he talked of empire, enthusing about the possibility that there would be a single empire parliament in London where a Canadian like he could serve one day. In the Jubilee pageant, followed by the scarlet-jacketed North-West Mounted Police, the Toronto Grenadiers with tall busbies, and the Royal Canadian Highlanders in kilts, he was recognized by the crowds and cheered second only to the queen herself. Reluctantly putting aside his egalitarian principles, he had accepted a knighthood the day before. He was no longer "Mr. Laurier," but "Sir Wilfrid." One British newspaper reported that he was "a politician of our New World . . . the equal of the great men of the Old Country."

Great Britain was Laurier's spiritual home. He admired British institutions, ideas, and literature, Britain's political tradition of individualism, and its legacy to Canada of liberty and tolerance. A "Liberal of the English school," he described himself with his habitual flourish. "I believe in that school which has all along claimed that it is the privilege of all subjects, whether high or low, whether rich or poor, whether ecclesiastics or laymen, to participate in the administration of public affairs, to discuss, to influence, to persuade, to convince—but which has always denied even to the highest the right to dictate even to the lowest." Canadians were "a free and happy people, and we are so owing to the liberal institutions by which we are governed, institutions which we owe to the exertions of our forefathers and the wisdom of the mother country."

National Archives of Canada C-81257

Laurier at the Jubilee.

Yet Laurier was a French Quebecer, worried that the excesses of Britain's imperialism could destroy the balance between the two language groups, overwhelming the minority of francophones struggling to exist in an Anglo-Saxon sea. He resisted efforts made by the British government in 1897 to bring Canada and the other self-governing colonies into a tighter relationship. He was consistent in his attitude to Britain throughout his long premiership; it became known as the policy of the "everlasting no."

Laurier's great ambition was "to consolidate Confederation, and to bring our people long-estranged from each other, gradually to become a nation. This is the supreme issue.

Everything else is subordinate to that idea." Canada had to be made strong enough, economically and politically, to have a life apart from Mother Britain. Sir John A. Macdonald's work of nation-building must be completed as a matter of urgency, before it all fell away. The challenge was to establish a consensus of moderate French and English opinion for sane national programs of the middle ground. The extremists could crusade on their own.

Laurier did not support the Confederation of four provinces into a federal union in 1867 because his French people were now surrounded by English speakers, with their different beliefs and priorities. Confederation would be the tomb of the French race. He was then in his late twenties—a lawyer and journalist, a French-Canadian nationalist, a critic of the Catholic Church, and just about to marry. He was part of a radical clique, but he was never a radical. Careful politics, not confrontation, were his way of making his ideas "triumph." The fight against the power of the church brought him into the Quebec legislature in 1871, but the stage and the issues were too small. A man who accepted reality, he was no longer an opponent of Confederation. As O.D. Skelton points out in *The Life and Letters of Sir Wilfrid Laurier,* his views had widened through the influence of English liberalism and contacts with English and French settlers near his home. "His sympathy with his own people never lessened, but he came to see that their future lay not in isolation, nor, for that matter, in assimilation, but in full and frank partnership with their fellow-Canadians."

Laurier entered the House of Commons in 1874. Within three years he was chosen to serve in the Alexander Mackenzie government. He became the dominant Liberal force in his province, and by 1887 he had taken over the entire party as leader of the opposition to Macdonald's Conservatives. He succeeded Edward Blake, who had to convince both him and the party that Laurier was the right person to confront the apparently unbeatable John A.

It was not self-evident. Before becoming federal Liberal leader, Laurier was a natural but unfocused politician. His animated resistance to the hanging of the half-French Louis Riel for treason in 1885 was an exception in a period when he often seemed uninterested and inactive. Frail since a young man, he suffered from severe bronchitis. He loved to be in his library, alone. He corresponded with Edward Blake in Greek, and a Liberal journalist, J.S. Willison, once overheard him discussing rare cookbooks with enthusiasm. Like Pierre Trudeau a century later, he valued the intellectual's life of contemplation, though he was easily dismissed as a dilettante, an amateur in politics. "Laurier will never make a leader; he has not enough of the devil in him," one Liberal complained. Another added concern about "his want of physical strength." "I know I have not the aptitude for it," the new chief admitted, "and I have a sad apprehension that it must end in disaster."

Initially, there was the predicted disaster. As a French Roman Catholic who had defended Riel, he was suspect in English Canada; as a politician who had shown a willingness to compromise for the sake of national unity, he was suspect in Quebec. He tried to scuttle Macdonald by promising a free trade pact with the Americans, but was trounced as a turncoat in the election of 1891. Only after the Grand Old Man's death did Laurier put his stamp on Canadian politics, crafting an economic stand not very different from the Conservatives' National Policy (but sounding distinct) and pumping up Liberal morale at the first national party convention ever held in Canada. With the Tories tied up in a dispute over religion

SUNNY WAYS AT WASHINGTON.

JOHN BULL—I don't know precisely what he may be after, Jonathan, but he'll get warrant.

and minority education rights in Manitoba, Laurier was an easy winner in the 1896 campaign.

Laurier soon demonstrated an instinct for power, patronage, and survival. In Willison's opinion, an admittedly biased one from a Liberal supporter, "the qualities of decision and resolution which Laurier possessed in such remarkable degree were those in which he was thought deficient. It is just as remarkable that despite his reputation for indolence, when he became Prime Minister he was an example of industry in office, indefatigable in his attendance in Parliament and diligent and vigorous in the direction of the party, which he recreated and over which he exercised such complete authority." "Reforms are for Oppositions," Laurier said bluntly. "It is the business of Governments to stay in office."

He promised to solve the Manitoba problem with "sunny ways," and did so immediately. The provincial government had thrown out the public funding of Catholic schools, which were populated mainly by a dwindling French minority. The federal government could order Manitoba to restore the Catholic system, but the new prime minister wanted nothing to do with coercion. Instead, he worked out a deal that gave something to both sides. French Catholics would receive religious education, but only within the public framework and on a limited basis. Their separate schools would not return. Laurier did not think that a necessity for the survival of his people. "Give our children the best education possible," he advised, "put them on an equal footing with those of the other race, and give them the legitimate pride which they will have in such a struggle." Historian Réal Bélanger, the author of a good biography of Laurier, is sure that he was "more a skilful politician than a sincere defender of the Catholic minority."

Laurier faced some of his greatest challenges and achieved some of his administration's longest-lasting accomplishments in the area of defence. The sorry state of the country's defences had been an issue in the election of 1896. A war scare during the winter of 1895–96, when an American attack on Canada appeared to be an immediate possibility, laid bare the utter inadequacy of Canada's militia force in equipment, training, and organization and discredited the previous

Conservative administration. Laurier appointed a committed reformer, Frederick W. Borden, to the defence portfolio. The prime minister supported Borden and gave him room to manoeuvre, so long as the costs were not excessive.

To defend Canada from threats outside and in, there were only a few professional soldiers, and their role was primarily as instructors for fewer than 40,000 part-time militia troops. There was little reason to do more, and good political motives for the prime minister to desist. The main argument for better military preparedness came from British leaders, who wanted Canadian help in warding off their potential enemies. This was a divisive appeal. Some English-speaking Canadians, many of British birth, wanted Canada to respond generously to the call. Others, especially the francophones who formed the bedrock of Laurier's support, had no interest in spending money and spilling blood to uphold British power. Those opposed to the British Empire accurately pointed out that Canada faced no important direct threats to its security. The only purpose of improved Canadian forces would be to provide cannon fodder for imperialistic British wars half way around the world, in areas of no concern to Canada.

Laurier confronted this sharp division of opinion in October 1899 with the outbreak of war in South Africa, a remote frontier of the empire. He got the news on the train back from Chicago from his travelling companion Willison, who told him he must send troops or get out of office right away. Laurier's reaction was to be "reluctant, unconvinced and rebellious." The pressure built from the British and English Canada, but also opposition from French Canada. The prime minister mastered the contradictory demands by agreeing that those who wished to serve could do so. Canada would raise units and transport them to South Africa, but they would then become

National Archives of Canada C-63517

Looking every bit the imperious ruler of Canada, Laurier cut a fine figure.

part of the British forces. Britain would pay for them.

Canada's initial, and largely symbolic, contribution of 1,000 troops ultimately grew to a total of nearly 8,000, as the expected early victory faded into a prolonged, costly three-year struggle. The Canadians served in nationally distinct units where good, often outstanding, performance in battle greatly increased their self-confidence, and that of their government. The war also raised nationalist and anti-imperialist opposition to Laurier in his home province. He lost his protégé, Henri Bourassa, who left the Liberal caucus. Bourassa said that the British would be back for more, and that Canadians should stand guard only on their native soil. Nevertheless, Laurier kept his Quebec support, winning easy victories in the elections of 1900 and 1904.

When the British pressed Laurier to carry on with permanent contributions to their forces after the South African War, he saw that this issue could prolong and widen the division in

Canadian opinion. He rejected such appeals, while supporting Borden's program for improvement and expansion of the country's own national forces. Canada would strengthen the empire, but only by improved self-defence that would relieve Britain's overstretched armed forces of North American commitments.

Among Laurier's important reforms was the Militia Act of 1904, opening the top appointment in the force for the first time to Canadian officers. Previously the senior position had always been reserved for a well-qualified British officer. This move delighted even his most bitter anti-imperial critics. In 1905 Laurier offered to replace the British troops at Halifax and Esquimalt with Canadian regulars. The cash-strapped British Army agreed, and the prime minister provided Canadian garrisons immediately, even though it was an expensive major commitment that required the government to triple the size of the Permanent Force to over 3,000 personnel and to greatly increase defence spending. In 1903 the defence budget had been $3.7 million; by 1907 it was $6.9 million.

The provision of the coastal garrisons was only the most dramatic part of the military reform that had begun in a small way during Laurier's first term and had gathered momentum during and after the South African War. The small permanent army did not just grow in size. It also began to acquire the technical and support services that were essential to sustain a modern military organization. These full-time professional cadres in turn helped to organize and train the necessary technical and support units in the part-time militia. Canada's military medical, engineering, and logistical services all trace their origins to the Laurier government's reforms.

The Laurier formula, then, was self-reliance, moderation, equilibrium, unity, and economic development—without that, there could be nothing in this young and fragile country. He was fortunate to govern in the best of times. Industry boomed, the wheat crop exploded, and immigration soared under government programs directed by Laurier's energetic interior minister, Clifford Sifton, the western heavyweight in the Cabinet. The government vigorously supported the National Policy of high tariffs while promoting empire trade, and it never completely closed the door on freer trade with the United States. International commercial agreements began to be negotiated separately from Britain. The new provinces of Alberta and Saskatchewan were created in 1905. The prime minister was even optimistic enough—too optimistic, as it proved—to approve two new transcontinental railways.

Laurier hit the high point of his popularity in the 1904 election. After that, it was downhill all the way, but slowly. Grievances from eight years of activism were piling up, scandals undermined the government, ministers grew weary, and the party was neglected. At his best, Laurier was a relaxed leader. "I'm a lazy dog," he would say disarmingly, and biographer Skelton points out that "he was not deeply and vitally interested in more than a few questions." He had an "easy-going trust." "He would often defer dealing with a rising question or disciplining a colleague whose public policy or private conduct called for a check, until a crisis forced action." Yet on some occasions he would ambush a minister with a cowardly *fait accompli*, as he did to Sifton in an attempt to entrench Catholic education rights in the new Alberta and Saskatchewan. Sifton resigned and Laurier back pedalled, asking his former minister to draft new clauses for the legislation and ensuring that the French minority received little. Nationalist opinion in Quebec groaned, but Laurier remained strong in the 1908 election, especially at home.

The prime minister's success with the army failed him when he tried to extend the formula from land to sea. Early in 1909 a panic swept Great Britain. It spread to Canada as well, thanks to the trans-ocean telegraphic cable. Germany, now Britain's principal competitor, was apparently expanding its naval program to gain superiority over the Royal Navy—the empire's first line of defence—in the crucial category of battleships, the largest and most powerful warships. Opinion in Canada split, as it always did when such fundamental questions burst forth urgently. At one extreme were Quebec nationalists, who insisted the country should do nothing, and at the other were English-Canadian imperialists, who believed the dominion should give direct help to the Royal Navy, perhaps in the form of a generous cash grant for battleship construction.

Laurier applied the same formula of support for increased national defence that had proved so effective in the controversies over land forces. Canada would now build a navy of its own, including eleven substantial sea-going warships. The Royal Canadian Navy, founded in 1910, was primarily intended for duty in Canadian waters, to relieve the British fleet of its residual responsibilities there. In the event of a crisis, the government could place Canadian ships under British command, subject to approval by Parliament.

Laurier's middle way satisfied few. French nationalists such as Henri Bourassa, who had been willing to support a national army on Canadian soil, charged that the navy would inevitably serve as a branch of the British fleet and be ordered away to fight remote wars on Britain's behalf. The Conservative Party pointed out that the Laurier navy did not provide the battleships Britain really needed, and in any event the new national service could not possibly be effective for many years to come, far too late for the crisis at hand. Tory leader Robert Borden forged an alliance, based solely on hatred for the Laurier policy, between nationalists in Quebec and

English-Canadian imperialists. This opposition cut deeply into the prime minister's support both in his province and in English-speaking constituencies.

In 1911 Laurier negotiated a trade agreement with the Americans which seemed likely to make the electorate forget his past sins. It was apparently the perfect deal, giving the increasingly numerous farmers of the West free trade in natural products, while retaining the high tariff barriers of the National Policy for the manufacturers of central Canada. But it all fell apart, and the Laurier government with it. Opposition from boards of trade, business, and the media rapidly built. Sifton and other prominent Liberals deserted the Laurier ranks. The prime minister was put on the defensive. Hardly able to believe his luck, Conservative leader Borden grew increasingly more confident. Obstruction in Parliament made Laurier think he had no escape but to call an election. He was and remains the only federal leader ever to take his majority government to the people after just three years.

It was a big mistake. Laurier and his tired old party were never able to regain the initiative. There

National Archives of Canada C-46319

Laurier in old age, with a young, ambitious Mackenzie King hovering over him.

was no way to counter arguments that the reciprocity pact was the first of several that would devastate the east-west economic links Canadians had built up so carefully. Or that the Liberals' intention was to remove Canada from the warmth of its traditional ties to Britain and to link the country in a political union with the United States. Weighed down by his navy in Quebec and reciprocity in English Canada, Laurier did his best to insist that he was not a traitor to his people or his country:

> I am branded in Quebec as a traitor to the French, and in Ontario as a traitor to the English. In Quebec I am branded as a Jingo, and in Ontario as a Separatist. In Quebec I am attacked as an Imperialist, and in Ontario as an anti-Imperialist. I am neither. I am a Canadian. Canada has been the inspiration of my life. I have had before me as a pillar of fire by night and a pillar of cloud by day a policy of true Canadianism, of moderation, of conciliation. I have followed it consistently since 1896, and I now appeal with confidence to the whole Canadian people to uphold me in this policy of sound Canadianism which makes for the greatness of our country and of the Empire.

In politics it is almost impossible to prove a negative. Laurier coaxed young people to "follow my white plume—the white hairs of sixty-nine years—and you will, I believe I can say it without boasting, find it always in the forefront of honour." But for the first time since 1896, the eloquence and the issues were not sufficient, and Canadians did not follow. Bourassa even saw to it that Laurier barely won Quebec.

As opposition leader, Laurier held the Liberals together into the First World War. He had no doubt it was a just cause or that Canadians ought to support it wholeheartedly. Despite the growing scepticism in Quebec about the war, he spoke to recruiting rallies, urging enlistment "that France may live, that

Britain may continue her noble and generous rule and that heroic Belgium may be restored to her standing as a nation." However, he broke with Prime Minister Borden and English members of his own party over conscription—compulsory military service for the country's young men. Laurier refused to enter into a coalition government with Borden, and he watched many of his English-Canadian members of parliament line up for conscription and against him.

In the election of 1917, the most racially divided in Canadian history, the Laurier Liberals won almost everything in Quebec but almost nothing outside. Laurier was not bitter. He wrote to a friend: "In the House, the few of us Liberals who have survived are all united. We have no ambition to defeat, even to harass the government. Quite the reverse: our only aim is to help and assist."

Laurier dominated the Liberal Party for more than three decades through extraordinary personal gifts. "He bamboozles me most sweetly, often," a journalist recounted. "I know when he does it, and he knows I know. Still I am bamboozled." But there was far more to it than that. Laurier's great charm stemmed from an ability to see the world as others saw it. He was genuinely not obsessed by power, status, or ego. After the conscription crisis, without rancour, he began to reconstruct the shattered Liberals, bringing them back together as a bicultural institution representative of the country as a whole. He saved the national party system from degenerating into ethnic factionalism, and prepared Liberalism to rule Canada for most of the twentieth century.

Sir Robert Borden

Brought to power almost by accident in the free-trade election of 1911, Robert Borden was a grim, unyielding, and sometimes inspired Canadian war leader. Victory was everything, however it was won, and there was nothing he would not do to achieve it. Linguistic unity, rural concerns, workers' needs—all had to be sacrificed to maintain the armies at the front. The First World War became Canada's war, and Borden insisted that the world recognize that the country was a colony no more.

Born in Grand Pré, Nova Scotia, June 26, 1854; died in Ottawa June 10, 1937. Prime minister for nine years: October 10, 1911–July 10, 1920

R obert Borden became Conservative Party leader in 1901 in the middle of the boom of Laurier Liberalism, and he made his reputation as a crusader for clean government. Sixteen years later, in the middle of the greatest war the world had ever seen, Borden's government would impose conscription to keep the strength of the Canadian Corps intact in the trenches. Then, to win the 1917 election, he altered the franchise, giving the vote to women relatives of soldiers (women, at that time, did not have the vote), taking it away from "enemy aliens," even those who had become citizens, and gerrymandering the soldiers' vote. The contradictions were obvious, the situational ethics clear. To Borden, the ends of victory justified the means, even if he alienated his party from Quebec on the conscription issue for a generation and more. Without victory overseas—and he believed conscription would contribute to that—everything would be lost. To achieve victory, he would do whatever was necessary.

A Nova Scotian, a Conservative, and a lawyer who had made his way by hard work and persistence, Borden found himself elected to Parliament from Halifax in 1896, the year the Conservatives were defeated. He sat in opposition while his party, led by Sir Charles Tupper, tried to cope with the charms and wiles of Prime Minister Wilfrid Laurier. Then, after the Liberals' re-election in 1900, Tupper had finally had enough. So bleak was the Tory situation that no one wanted the job of leader. To his surprise, Borden found himself pushed forward. He agreed, but only for a short period.

He remained almost twenty years. Repeatedly, challengers stepped forward; repeatedly, Borden offered to resign, only to see other contenders neutralize each other and leave him in place. So Borden kept the job, inspiring almost no one in his party or in the country. In 1904, crusading against corruption and patronage, he led his party to fewer seats than Tupper had won in 1900. In 1908, standing on a markedly progressive platform he had enunciated at Halifax the year before, he picked up ten seats, but had to face down still more discontent in caucus. He was a lovely fellow, Ontario MP Sam Hughes said of his leader, but he lacked "political guts." Borden's wife said he had her permission to get out of politics—"and fast." But he survived, and soon enough his moment in history arrived.

The Liberals seemed to have taken the day, or so everyone believed when a reciprocity agreement with the United States was introduced into the House of Commons in 1911. The negotiations, conducted in secret, surprised the country, but it was the nature of the terms that left Borden and his caucus stunned in their seats. William Fielding, the finance minister, read out the clauses that seemed to open the US market to Canadian farmers, yet still protect Canadian industry. Borden was shattered—until his MPs returned to their constituencies to discover that manufacturers feared this deal was the thin edge of a wedge towards a continentalism that would bankrupt them. Other MPs heard their voters mutter that the Catholic French-speaking Laurier had sold out the empire, tying Canada to the Americans.

There were ways to fight reciprocity, and Borden set out to exploit them by means that would have done Sir John A. proud. First, and most important, he struck a written deal with key manufacturers, almost all Toronto Liberals, to "bust the damn thing" and put key business representatives into his Cabinet should he win the election. Then he made an arrangement with the *nationaliste* Henri Bourassa to have their parties stay out of each other's ridings in Quebec. It wasn't free trade that worried Bourassa so much as Laurier's "soft on the empire" attitudes, and he was willing to collaborate with Borden, a traditional imperialist, to help destroy the prime minister.

And it worked. Laurier's men, who had thought they had a winning issue in reciprocity, found themselves instead fighting for their lives against the country's manufacturers, the newspapers they controlled, and the Quebec nationalists. The Tories, for their part, were flush with contributions from business, had a host of provincial governments working with them, and had organized the party well. Borden's patriotic speeches helped: "I believe that we are . . . standing today at the parting of the ways . . . We must decide whether the spirit of Canadianism or of Continentalism shall prevail on the northern half of this continent." The voters chose Borden and Canadianism, a smashing victory for him.

Getting power proved easier than making good use of it. The strains within the Borden government were real. The Quebec Conservatives, or *bleus*, were suspicious of Borden's imperialism, especially when he offered to make a $35 million contribution to the Royal Navy, sufficient to build three dreadnaughts. The big-gun ships were the winning weapon of the era, and Germany was in a race for supremacy with the Royal Navy. Yet the costs were huge in an era of small government, and Quebec Tories were outraged. Their chief, Frederick Monk, resigned from the Cabinet. The Liberal Senate killed the deal, but it left francophones deeply wounded. The Orange and anti-Catholic sympathies of Sam Hughes, the minister of militia, were constantly on display, and in ways that dampened the military ardour of Quebec

Sir Robert Borden

National Archives of Canada C-9259

PUNCH, OR THE LONDON CHARIVARI.—July 17, 1912.

THE KNIGHT OF THE MAPLE-LEAF.

SIR BORDEN. "Lady, an there be an Armageddon or other scrap toward, count me in!"
BRITANNIA. "Sir, I could desire no better champion!"

militiamen. The weak economy did its share too, as unemployment rose and trade slowed. Tory times, the Liberals jeered, were hard times.

The war that began in August 1914 tested Borden and the country to the limit. Canada had no share in the decision-making preceding the conflict, nor, as a colony, did it have any right to declare war or stay neutral. When Britain went to war, Canada was at war. All Borden could decide was how generous a contribution his country would make, and there was no doubt in his mind or in those of English Canadians.

He would do his utmost for the empire and, through the empire, for Canada.

The first contingent, conjured up from the militia, old soldiers, and volunteers, was gathered together with remarkable speed at Valcartier, Quebec, and shipped off to England within weeks of Britain's declaration of war. Borden armed his government with a new War Measures Act that gave the Cabinet full power to do whatever it wished, and for a time the Liberals cheered the government. But soon stories of patronage running rampant began to appear, along with charges of profiteering: boots that leaked, rifles that didn't fire, horses with broken backs—and all the profits going to friends of the government. For a proponent of clean government, Borden's response was unaccountably weak, and it took two years to get rid of Hughes, a minister who was sane only part of the time, and his corrupt cronies. There were huge financial difficulties as the costs of the war escalated.

National Archives of Canada C–46314

The prime minister, taking the salute from a passerby on Parliament Hill.

The railways were another colossal problem. Canada had too many railways, all financed with government money and with publicly sold shares. Now markets were in difficulty, and the war was dislocating everything. Soon the railways, vital to move supplies and men, were teetering on the edge, and Borden had to find some way of dealing with the mess. His solution—a royal commission—delayed the crisis.

It was manpower that most bedevilled the prime minister. The simple truth was that the casualties at the front were horrific, literally inconceivable. The demands for more men were never-ending. Borden was unimpressed by the British generals who sent tens of thousands to their deaths against German machine-guns and uncut barbed wire. He warned Britain's prime minister, David Lloyd George, that if the slaughter caused by incompetent military leadership went on, "not a Canadian soldier will leave the shores of Canada so long as the Canadian people entrust the government of their country to my hands."

But the war had to be won. At the end of 1915 Borden had made a "sacred pledge" that Canada would put a half-million into the field. None of his ministers had been consulted, but Borden's promise came to be seen as binding on the country. The problem was that British-born Canadians had rushed to the colours, and, though the native-born Anglo Canadians were slower, tens of thousands were enlisting by 1916. French Canadians, however, hung back. The real threat to their interests, Montreal newspapers claimed, was not from Prussia but from the Huns of Ontario, who were closing French schools. The political mood in Quebec was openly anti-war. Borden, who understood very little about French Canada, did nothing to try to change minds; his Cabinet, very weak in its Quebec ministers, did no better. Unlike Macdonald, Borden could never find a Quebec lieutenant. No one was surprised at his failure, for he believed that "the vision of the French Canadian is very limited."

Pressure from English Canada mounted for what was called, in a horrible phrase, "equality of sacrifice." French Canadians must be made to enlist and die in the same proportion. How could that be done? The only way was conscription, drafting men into the Canadian Expeditionary Force to serve in the trenches of France and Flanders. Borden was loath to make this order, for he could see the turmoil it would cause in Quebec, with organized labour, and with farmers, but over time his attitudes hardened. "It may be necessary to resort to compulsion," he wrote a supporter at the beginning of 1917. "I hope not; but if the necessity arises I shall not hesitate to act accordingly." The war in 1916 had been in stalemate, but by 1917, with revolutionary Russia on the verge of leaving the war, the Allies were losing. The time had come.

Borden went to Britain and France in early 1917 to see for himself and to participate in the Imperial War Conference with British and dominion leaders. He was appalled by the terrible casualties on the Somme battlefields—Britain had lost more than 400,000 men and Canada 24,000—and impressed by the need for more men. He insisted that because Canada had put a corps of four divisions in the field, the nation was entitled to more say than it had been granted in determining the direction of the war. His efforts led to Resolution IX at the War Conference, which asserted dominion rights in foreign policy. Borden, remarkably, had won Canada near-equality with the mother country and, as the South African prime minister Jan Christian Smuts noted, he had changed the empire.

If Canada was equal, however, it must, as a sovereign nation, act to maintain its armies at strength. When Borden returned to Canada in May 1917, he came determined to impose conscription. First, he tried to persuade Laurier to join him in a government committed to compulsory service, but Laurier refused. Then he began to explore the support of other Liberals. The initial soundings were coolly received; not even the passage of the Military Service Act moved the Grits. What did shake them loose from their partisan allegiance were two pieces of legislation: the Military Voters Act allowed soldiers' votes to be allocated almost at will to constituencies that needed them to elect conscriptionists; and the Wartime Elections Act gave the vote to women who would support conscription, and took it away from the dubious foreign-born naturalized citizens. These acts were largely the handiwork of the Manitoban Arthur Meighen, who day by day was becoming Borden's strongest minister.

The elections acts, pieces of shameless gerrymandering unworthy of a democratic government, frightened the Liberals out of their political wits. As Borden wrote in his diary in September, "I am beginning to feel that we should take them in as our first duty is to win, at any cost, the coming election in order that we may continue to do our part in winning the war and that Canada not be disgraced." Helped by Meighen, Borden put together his Union Government the next month, a combination of federal Conservatives and Liberals drawn largely from provincial governments. In every way that mattered the ruthless and victory-determined Borden had welded together a coalition of English-speaking Tories and Liberals to implement conscription—and, critics charged then and later, to settle the problem of Canada's bankrupt railways by nationalizing all but the profitable Canadian Pacific into one government-run line. Against them stood Laurier, with a few loyal English-speaking followers and a united French Canada.

The election of 1917 was the dirtiest in Canadian history.

The Union campaign painted Laurier as a traitor who, if he won, would do so leading the cockroaches of the kitchen of Canada to victory. "A vote for Laurier," the hitherto Liberal *Manitoba Free Press* editorialized, "is a vote for the Kaiser." Nothing was held back. The farmers, who feared that conscription would strip them of the labour they needed to bring in their crops, were promised exemptions—two weeks before the vote. The result was a Borden coalition landslide, with Laurier supreme only in Quebec.

Canada was divided as never before. The government called up the men for the army, and 99 percent of Québécois sought exemption. Dreadful as that sounded, in Ontario, 95 percent tried to be excused from military service. When, in March 1918, the Germans launched a great and successful offensive in France and Flanders, Borden panicked and cancelled the exemptions he had promised to the farmers before the election. Outraged to lose their sons and labourers just before planting season, the farmers marched on Ottawa, but got nowhere. Conscription was popular only with those who were too young or too old for the front. Given the casualties overseas, this reaction may have been understandable, but Borden stubbornly persisted. By late 1918 he had his 100,000 conscripts overseas or en route to the trenches. The Canadian Expeditionary Force, its four divisions up to strength, over 350,000 men in its ranks, and its morale sky-high, played a critical role as the shock troops of the Allied armies. But 60,000 dead, and countless thousands more wounded or maimed in spirit, were a high price to pay.

By war's end, Borden was weary of politics. He attended the Peace Conference in Paris to ensure that Lloyd George and the leaders of the other Great Powers recognized Canada's contribution in accord with the newly won dominion rights in foreign policy, and he did get substantial

recognition. Canada signed the Treaty of Versailles. Borden's signature, along with those of the other dominion prime ministers, followed that of the British leader. Borden won Canada a seat in the League of Nations and the right of election to its Council. These major steps towards autonomy and independence were achieved over the opposition of the United States, which saw Canada and the other dominions as just more British votes at the League it would eventually decline to join.

When Borden returned to Canada from France in late May 1919, he found the country in a near-revolutionary state. The workers of Winnipeg were in the midst of a huge general strike that would be broken only by the army and the Royal North-West Mounted Police. Socialist and communist rhetoric filled the union halls and resonated at street corners. Unrest was everywhere, inflation was soaring, and returned men, as the veterans were called, had no jobs, no housing, and scant benefits from an ungrateful nation. The farmers, disillusioned by the government's elimination of their exemptions from conscription and fearful that the postwar period would see business entrench the high tariffs that raised the cost of goods, were organizing themselves into the Progressive Party. Ontario, stalwart, rock-ribbed, conservative Ontario, elected a farmer-labour government in October 1919. Borden could look at the Prairies and Ontario—and even into his Maritimes—to see that federal Conservatives would have a hard time in the next election. It was depressing to a man who had become heartily sick of politics. Worn out, fatigued, the complaints of Canadians grating on his ears, Borden simply could not summon the energy to try to deal with the aftermath of the war.

Then there was Quebec. Borden's desultory efforts to forge an alliance with francophone high-tariff politicians and businessmen went nowhere. Conscription and his anti-French 1917 election campaign hung round his neck like an albatross. The Conservative Party would need more than a generation to recover from Borden's policies towards Quebec.

By December 1919 Borden was sick and tired. His doctor said he had to retire, but the Union caucus refused to accept his resignation. There was no obvious or popular successor. Borden took a long vacation that kept him away until May 1920, then resigned on July 1.

The outgoing leader now set out to find his replacement. The Liberals had picked Mackenzie King as Laurier's successor in August 1919 in a great national convention that adopted a social welfare platform. The Tories and Borden made their choice in the back rooms, consulting party nabobs and the caucus. The Cabinet favoured the finance minister, Sir Thomas White, and so initially did Borden. The wartime money-raising minister was not only competent but popular, despite having imposed the nation's first income tax, but he, too, was worn down by his nine years in office and declined to lead the government. The Union caucus wanted the acerbic minister of the interior, Arthur Meighen, and Borden, who greatly admired the young minister's abilities, agreed that the Manitoban was the best choice.

Borden was gone, to the relief of Quebec and the cheers of a few supporters. He had been a middlingly successful party leader from 1901 to 1911, and a weak prime minister from 1911 to 1914 or 1915. But during the dark days of the war, his grim determination to prevail, to do everything that was needed to secure victory, showed the man's true grit. In 1921, the journalist Augustus Bridle summed up the prevailing view of that day: "Canada had never before had a mediocrity of such eminence; a man without a spark of genius devoted a high talent to a nation's work so well that he just about wins a niche in our Valhalla—if we have one. It was the war that almost finished Borden and it was the war that made him."

True enough, it was the war that made Borden's reputation, for good and ill. He had made the First World War into Canada's war, but he divided Canada along racial and regional lines, pitted French against English, urban against rural Canada, labour and capital against each other, and he left the nation strained and sore. No prime minister in our history before or since left his country so divided. Whatever else he was, Borden was no Macdonald, no leader who could jolly the country along with him. Worse still, Meighen, his successor, was the worst possible choice for a leader to bind up the wounds. Power in Canada waited for the leader who could.

Arthur Meighen

Canada's greatest political orator, Arthur Meighen, could stir a crowd, but he could never command loyalty among workers, westerners, or Quebecers. Intelligent but blinkered, he carried out Borden's toughest tasks and became prime minister with his enemies ready made. A master of everything but politics, Meighen failed as prime minister because he could never undo his past record or steer a course that appealed to the majority.

Born in St. Mary's, Ontario, June 16, 1874; died in Toronto, August 5, 1960. Prime minister for two years: July 10, 1920–December 29, 1921; June 29, 1926–September 25, 1926

Arthur Meighen's roots were in Northern Ireland, and he inherited the fierce political and sectarian passions that bedevilled the British province. He grew up in rural Ontario, the son of the first schoolmaster in the little town of St. Mary's. There he was force-fed the same Anglo-Saxon small-town and rural virtues of hard work, diligence, duty, and loyalty to queen and empire that characterized most of Canada's English-speaking leaders. Meighen was bright, a good student, and he attended St. Mary's Collegiate—a choice that immediately separated him from most young boys of his age who left school at the earliest opportunity. He excelled in mathematics, which appealed to his ordered mind, and he was a natural debater, again applying his instinctive logician's skills to the strict rules of formal debate. Then in 1892 he enrolled at the University of Toronto where Meighen, quiet and competent, seemed to live in the shadow of other more gregarious students. One was William Lyon Mackenzie King, a campus politician and leader of a notorious student strike, who had his eye fixed firmly on his guiding star.

Meighen's family was not well off. After graduation he clerked in a store, then went to normal school to qualify as a teacher. His first experiences in a classroom revealed much about the man. When he expelled the daughter of the school board's chairman, Meighen held his ground in the explosion that followed. Either he or the chairman could win that fight, and it was not the new schoolmaster. Through with teaching, Meighen moved west in 1899 to Portage la Prairie, Manitoba, and to law. After a period of apprenticeship, he married a schoolteacher and his career flourished. His oratory and logic came together in the courtroom, and he quickly made a name for himself. The chance to go to Parliament followed soon after when the Conservative nomination was his for the taking. He took it, ran in the 1908 election, and, to his astonishment, won. Arthur Meighen, MP, sounded very sweet to a failed schoolteacher and small-town lawyer.

The Conservatives were in opposition, led in a lacklustre way by Robert Borden, who butted his party's head against the seemingly unstoppable Liberal machine of Sir Wilfrid Laurier. An unknown back-bencher, Meighen could have said nothing and watched. But that was not his style, and soon his oratory rang out in the Commons. He used his logic to pin down government ministers, his sarcasm to score political points, his relentlessness to hound the government front bench until they all but begged for mercy. The story has it that the prime minister, watching Meighen deliver his maiden speech, turned to his seatmate and said, "Borden has found a man." True enough, and when Borden won the 1911 election, he had his eye on young Meighen.

There was no immediate seat in the Cabinet, however, and Meighen spent two years chafing with impatience. Not until 1913, after he had distinguished himself with his brilliant speeches in defence of the new government's naval policy, did Borden make him solicitor general, the most junior of portfolios. Once war began in August 1914, Borden turned more and more to the indefatigable Manitoban to draft legislation, defend government policies, and offer the advice he wanted to hear. It was Meighen's fertile brain in 1917 that dreamed up the basic tenets of the Wartime Elections Act—to give the vote to female relatives of soldiers and take it away from recent "enemy alien" immigrants to Canada. It was Meighen who worked out the details of the Military Voters Act—to let soldiers vote for the government or the opposition and to have their ballots allocated to the ridings where the government most needed them. It was Meighen who drafted much of the Military Service Act, the measure that imposed conscription on the country to feed the insatiable demands of the trenches for more men. In 1919, it was Meighen who

National Archives of Canada C-29632

shaped the Borden government's tough response to the Winnipeg General Strike. The war had to be won, and anything that helped to that end was justified. The nation had to have order, and the workers could not paralyze the operations of a large city with a major strike. To Meighen, these were certitudes.

None of these measures won universal praise. Labour hated Meighen for his role in crushing the Winnipeg strike, French Canada despised him for conscription, and the Liberals believed he had stolen the 1917 election by corrupting politics. To Robert Borden, however, Meighen was the one minister he could rely on to find a way, the minister who would always do what was needed. When Borden, exhausted by the burdens of wartime leadership, gave up the reins in July 1920, it was to Meighen that he turned to succeed him.

The new leader faced huge problems of an unprecedented severity. His political enemies were legion. The economy, struggling to emerge from wartime inflation and the disruption of global trade, was in a perilous condition. Quebec regarded him and his party with loathing. The farmers were in political revolt, turning their backs on the old parties and demanding progressive legislation, not least in a broad lowering of tariffs.

Perhaps no one could have led the government to victory, but Meighen certainly made a hash of it. He offered no gestures to Quebec or to labour, for the tactics of brokerage politics—something for everyone—had no appeal to a man with principled positions on every issue. He made no attempt to mollify farmers who objected to the protective tariffs that favoured central Canadian manufacturers at their expense. Characteristically, Meighen apologized for nothing. Conscription had been necessary, he lectured audiences in Quebec. Putting down the Winnipeg General Strike was the sole alternative to anarchy. High tariffs were essential if Canada was to have a strong manufacturing industry. Sounding not unlike Alexander Mackenzie fifty years before, Meighen pronounced the old ways, the old virtues, best. If Canadians wanted soft policies, they could vote for the leader of the Liberal Party, Mackenzie King, Meighen's despised classmate from university days.

Of course, they did. Meighen led his party to a dismal third-place finish in the general election in December 1921, falling behind the Progressives, as the loosely organized farmers called themselves, and the Liberals, who formed the government. In opposition through what soon became the booming twenties, Meighen continued on the offensive. He spoke for imperial loyalty, called for the maintenance of the tariff, and denounced King at every turn. There were no gestures to the Progressives, whose party links were fraying visibly day by day, though King took every advantage he could of their weakness. Still, King was no great leader himself in his first term and his inert Cabinet was wracked with scandals. There lay the opportunity, and Meighen soon established his dominance in the Commons. King presented few policies, and the Tory leader savaged him: "The Government shirks its responsibility, saying 'we have no opinion, or we have two opinions, or ten opinions, and cannot get together, and, therefore, we will wash our hands of the whole thing, and whatever parliament says we will do.'"

In the 1925 election Meighen made an extraordinary comeback, at least the equal of Macdonald's in 1878: he won the most seats, but too few for a majority. Banking on support from the Progressives, who had been reduced to twenty seats but held the balance of power, King stayed in office, determined to prove that he could govern. For a time he did, but Meighen was everywhere, his acerbic speeches flaying the Liberal front-benchers. On the critical vote of confidence, King lost narrowly. Instead of visiting the governor general, Lord Byng, and surrendering power to Meighen, the leader of the largest party, King asked for a new election. The governor general refused and called on Meighen to take the helm. After a few days of political chaos and a defeat in the House of Commons on a motion of non-confidence, Byng gave Meighen the dissolution he had refused King. The governor general handed the Liberal the political issue he needed.

The election turned on Byng's interference with the will of the people. At least, that was how King presented it. The Conservative leader argued in his speeches that this was nonsense, that Byng had been perfectly correct in his actions, and that Liberal corruption and incompetence were what mattered. The constitutional experts then and later made it clear that Byng and Meighen were in the right on the question of the dissolution of Parliament, but King turned the issue to his advantage. Was Canada willing to let an appointed British lord determine her destiny? Besides, though far from a giant, King had demonstrated that he was more than flexible enough to satisfy local and regional needs. Meighen was likely the "better" man, but he was so fixed in his views, so convinced he was right, so unwilling to bind up the nation's wounds, and so authoritarian in his approach that he frightened voters. It was King again when the ballots were counted, and Meighen, who lost his own seat in Portage la Prairie, soon retired from politics.

He was not yet gone forever. R.B. Bennett, his successor as party leader and in 1930 the prime minister, named him to the Senate. Meighen's speeches again rang through Parliament. In November 1941, with Canada at war and the Conservative Party all but leaderless, a party meeting called on Meighen to fight Mackenzie King once more. Meighen was willing. His policy was conscription, the only way he could conceive of fighting a war. But in a by-election in the safe Toronto constituency of South York, Meighen's rigidity ran into the electorate's desire that a better Canada emerge from the hell of war. Meighen fought against a CCF candidate and social welfare won, much to Mackenzie King's relief and Meighen's disgust. "There are an incredible number of people in these days," he complained, "who have the idea that all . . . troubles can be cured by the simple process of the Government distributing money here, there, and everywhere."

Bitter, convinced that the people had chosen fools to lead them, fearful of the loss of the old values, Meighen was at last through with politics. Ultimately, his record in politics and as prime minister was completely undistinguished. He had great gifts and a powerful mind, and he was one of the best political orators the country ever produced. Yet he failed to realize that Canada was a nation of regions and races, and he could never bring himself to bend his fixed principles to satisfy enough voters to win and hold power. He "strode up the bare staircase of his duty," his friend Eugene Forsey noted with exactitude, "uncheered and undismayed."

William Lyon Mackenzie King

Sly and tough, a master of timing and applied ruthlessness, Mackenzie King ruled Canada longer than anyone else, leaving his "government party" in command after his retirement. Few loved or admired him, but he accomplished much: he maintained cooperation between French and English Canadians, cut the tight bonds to the British Empire, established the welfare state, and, above all, provided superb leadership to a strong Canada through the Second World War.

Born in Berlin (Kitchener), Ontario, December 17, 1874; died in Kingsmere, Quebec, July 22, 1950. Prime minister for twenty-two years: December 29, 1921–June 28, 1926; September 25, 1926–August 6, 1930; October 23, 1935–November 15, 1948

"An orangutang that would flatter him could name its own reward," a hostile journalist observed of Mackenzie King in the 1920s. A speechwriter, quitting in disgust in the 1940s, admitted that he was tired of being midwife to an intellectual virgin. Poet Dennis Lee said King "sat in the middle and played with string" and "loved his mother like anything." The ultimate judgement on Mackenzie King, however, came from Norman Lambert, one of his key election operatives. Talking in 1941 to a Winnipeg journalist, he said he simply could not stand "the worm at close quarters—bad breath, a fetid unhealthy atmosphere, like living close to some filthy object. But get off a piece and he looks better." Up close, King's actions—and King himself—were often unimpressive. With perspective and time, however, the grand pattern emerges: Mackenzie King was Canada's greatest prime minister, party leader, and politician.

Mackenzie King was the first son and second child of the ineffectual John King, a law lecturer and author, and his wife, Isabel, the daughter of the Upper Canadian rebel of 1837, William Lyon Mackenzie. Born in exile in the United States, King's mother was the dominant personality in the household, and she filled her son with a powerful belief in himself and a need to vindicate her father's cause—to fight against Toryism, imperialism, and privilege.

Mackenzie King was a bright and able student who

attended the universities of Toronto, Chicago, and Harvard, eventually emerging with a BA, a law degree, two MAs, and a PhD. Short, stocky, moon-faced, he developed a predilection for rescue work with fallen women, with "strolls" and "wasted time"—phrases from King's diary that some have interpreted as sessions with prostitutes, though they might just as easily have been voyeurism, simple time-wasting, or failed efforts at social work. Whatever he did on these occasions, the important point is that King was never able to form a serious attachment that culminated in marriage. His and his mother's expectations of the "right" woman never coincided.

King's early career focused on social questions, on the conditions of workers and the poor. That interest turned into a government research job, thanks to family connections, and in 1900 King became deputy minister in the new Department of Labour. Over the next eight years he established a reputation as a labour expert and gravitated towards politics, running and winning as a Liberal in his home town. A year later, Laurier named him labour minister. King was a good, tireless Cabinet minister, and ambitious too, in his own mind the all-but-designated successor to Sir Wilfrid. When the Laurier government campaigned for reciprocity in 1911 and was defeated by the Conservative Party under Robert Borden, King himself lost his seat.

The next eight years were difficult. He became a consultant on labour questions in the employ of John D. Rockefeller Jr. and the Rockefeller Foundation, particularly with regard to the troubles that began in 1913 in the Colorado coalfields. King's first priority was his employer's interests: he established company unions and a policy of conciliation; improvements in working conditions came second. The salary he received from the Rockefellers was fabulous by the standards of the day, and the connections established were lifelong. During the

National Archives of Canada C-55540

The dog-loving King with 'Pat.'

First World War, however, King's work in the United States seemed unpatriotic. Why was he not in the army? For him, there was no difficulty in dealing with this question. He was forty years old in 1914, his parents were old and ill, and he had to help support his sisters. Still, his concern about appearances led King to a near breakdown in 1916, a crisis for which he sought psychological assistance at Johns Hopkins hospital in Baltimore, Maryland. Once he recovered, he tried to keep his name forward in Canadian politics by running in the 1917 election in North York, Ontario. When the Liberal Party split on Borden's Union government of conscriptionists, King decided to remain with Laurier. That loyalty would pay off handsomely.

The end of the Great War, with its terrible casualties and dislocation, produced unprecedented labour unrest in Canada. Mackenzie King was genuinely knowledgable in the area, and in 1918 he published a long tome on the subject, *Industry and Humanity*. Industrialists had the duty to deal humanely with workers, he argued. The book, with incomprehensible foldout charts and prose dripping with religious intensity, sold well, but remained largely unread.

Laurier died in February 1919 and the Winnipeg General

Strike erupted in May. King seemed to be the man of the hour as Liberals gathered in convention to select a new party leader. There were other better-known candidates, but King was the youngest and ablest, a Laurier loyalist, and a man with solid, constructive ideas on the great issue of the day—the relations between labour and capital. The party platform written at the convention (with King's fingerprints all over it) was reformist in its call for a social welfare state. King helped his cause immeasurably with a speech that brought the cheering audience to its feet. Shrewdly, he offered a panegyric to Laurier: "The questions we are discussing here are bound up with the great principle to the maintenance of which he gave his life, for which he fought all his political battles—yes, and for which he died; namely, the right of the people to control the Parliament of their country." The issue of the leadership was sealed when the Quebec delegates, marshalled in King's support by Ernest Lapointe, voted for him en bloc, though it took three ballots to determine the outcome.

King's task as Liberal leader was multifaceted. He had to reunite the Liberals' conscriptionist and anti-conscriptionist wings, in effect its English-Canadian and Quebec members. He had to keep a light in the window so that Liberalism could remain the ultimate home for restive farmers, then beginning to organize themselves into a separate, if loosely constructed, Progressive Party. He had to develop a tariff policy that had an appeal to the farmers, yet did not alienate the industrial interests of central Canada. He had to devise a reformist policy to show workers that his party could deal with their needs. He had to defeat the Union Government. Above all, he had to demonstrate that he was a leader, a man with the capacity to inspire his caucus and the country.

King worked tirelessly to rebuild his party. His image as a vigorous reformer appealed to many, though not to farmers.

In 1921 King ran against the Union Government's record and, like Macdonald and Laurier before him, presented himself as a conciliator, the man to bring together French and English Canadians, East and West, farmer, worker, and industrialist. King's message worked, and the Liberals captured 116 seats (including all sixty-five in Quebec), the Progressives sixty-four, and Meighen's tattered coalition fifty in a House of Commons of 235. King had won, but, with the first minority government in Canadian history, he would be forced to rely on the Progressives to govern. His political skills would be tested to the limit.

King held out an olive branch to the Progressives, trying to bring them into his Cabinet from the outset. When this effort failed, he began to offer small concessions on tariffs—the government's industrial supporters in central Canada were certain to object to anything larger—and to lower railway freight rates to seduce the farmers back to Liberalism. The Progressive leader, T.A. Crerar, a former Liberal and Unionist, left his quarrelsome colleagues and eventually entered King's Cabinet. Political seduction, it was obvious now, was King's stock in trade, and pragmatism and compromise his weapons. The laisser-faire legislative record of his first government was unimpressive, but King had again made the Liberal Party into an agency of French-English reconciliation as it had been under Sir Wilfrid. He had also gone a substantial distance in bringing farmers back to his side. Still, many observers thought that King was the personification of the procrastinator. His leadership appeared so weak that he acquired the jeering nickname of "Willy of the Valley."

At the same time and early in his career, King had his greatest success on the international stage. He was a strong supporter of British ideals and the monarchy, but a bristling opponent of arrogant Whitehall interference with Canada's autonomy. In 1922 Prime Minister David Lloyd George publicly asked for Canadian support for British forces at the Dardanelles seaport of Chanak, pinned down by the Turks, even before any request reached King. He was privately outraged at this assertion of an imperial foreign policy, but in public he said only that Parliament would decide. Parliament was not in session, of course, so no decision was forthcoming. Angered by the assumptions common in London, King arrived at the Imperial Conference of 1923 determined to get Canadian autonomy recognized: as a self-governing dominion, Canada had to make its own policy. Foreign Secretary Lord Curzon found the Canadian leader "obstinate, tiresome and stupid," but King prevailed. In 1926 the new relationship was recognized formally, though it was not put into law until the passage of the Statute of Westminster in 1931: the dominions were "autonomous Communities within the British Empire, equal in status, in no way subordinate to one another in any aspect of their domestic or external affairs, though united by a common allegiance to the Crown, and freely associated as members of the British Commonwealth of Nations." King's stubbornness and insistence on making foreign-policy decisions in Canada had begun to change the empire into the Commonwealth.

At home, however, King's government was in difficulty. In the 1925 election King seemed smugly satisfied with the stability he had brought to the country, and his campaign was as uninspired as the "common-sense" tariff he called for. The results shocked him: Meighen won seventeen seats more than King. His hold on the Liberal leadership seemed increasingly shaky, and he had even lost his own seat. To almost everyone's astonishment, King decided to try to govern on the assumption that he could get the support of the Progressives. This was his constitutional right, but the governor general, Viscount Byng, fumed that King had not behaved as a gentleman should.

In addition to this shaky hold on power, a major scandal was developing in the Customs Department, where the minister seemed to be directly enmeshed in bribery and graft. King tried to keep the Progressive and labour MPs on side by supporting old age pensions and by lowering taxes, but the scandal, investigated by a parliamentary committee, implicated two successive customs ministers. Facing defeat on a motion of censure, King went to Byng to seek a dissolution and the right to call another election. He had governed successfully for nine months, he told the governor general, and, believing he could still command a majority in Parliament, he argued that he was entitled to get what he asked for. Byng disagreed, refused King's request, and decided that Meighen must get a chance to govern. Gambling everything, King promptly resigned. There was no longer a prime minister, he told Parliament, a violation of the convention of parliamentary government that held that the nation could not be without a government. The next day, Meighen took office. But, using trickery and brilliant argumentation, the determined King forced a vote of confidence and won by one vote. Meighen quickly received the dissolution Byng had earlier refused King.

The election of 1926 decided whether King or Meighen, the Liberals or the Conservatives, would make the century theirs. King attacked Byng's refusal to grant him a dissolution: by what right did a British-appointed official interfere in the operations of Canada's democracy? The King-Byng wingding confused many with its muddy constitutional arguments, but King's Canadian nationalism struck a chord in Quebec and the West. More to the point, perhaps, Meighen's stern Ulster righteousness did not, and the election was a solid Liberal victory. King had a comfortable majority with 128 seats. The gamble had paid off handsomely, and Waffling Willie now seemed a man of decisiveness.

In his second administration, King presided over a country that was happily enjoying the booming twenties. Canada celebrated the Diamond Jubilee of Confederation in 1927, radio became popular, and King's Scottish burr was heard across the land. But when the economy took a sharp downturn in the fall of 1929, he missed its significance, as he viewed the decline as a normal cyclical event. King himself made a rare political error when he said in Parliament that he would not give one cent to any Tory provincial government. "I would not give them a five-cent piece," he went on, instantly knowing that he had made a huge mistake. The unemployed, people on relief, and the press in the seven provinces that did not have Liberal governments were furious, and in the election of 1930 King lost badly to the Tory, R.B. Bennett.

Perhaps King had been lucky to lose when he did. So powerful was his later reputation for political omniscience that the legend of a deliberate defeat developed. The Depression devastated both the land and the Bennett government. Not even the revelations of a huge Liberal scandal over hydroelectric power contracts, which plunged King and his party fundraisers into what he called the "Valley of Humiliation," did much to make the Conservative government look good. All King's eccentricities erupted in opposition. He fretted over his legacy, worried about his own solitary life, dabbled seriously in spiritualism, engaged in table-rapping sessions with mediums, and became obsessed over the arrangement of tea-leaves in his cup or soap in his shaving mug. Troubled as he was, however, he was not crazy, and he understood that it was simply a matter of waiting for the next

King addressing the nation on the sixtieth
anniversary of Confederation, 1927.

election. Though offering no policies of any substance in
1935, King won a huge majority, the biggest to that point. By
then, running against Bennett, he could not have lost.

King was now in his sixty-first year, but he remained vigorous and alert. His record as party leader through sixteen years
had been superb, if it was measured by building and holding
together a disparate coalition. His public record, aside from
his successes in strengthening Canada's autonomous place
within the Commonwealth, was weak. There had been no
great achievements, no attempt, the insubstantial Old Age
Pensions legislation notwithstanding, to put into law the
reform platform of 1919 to which King's party had committed itself. But as fate had it, King would have thirteen more
years in power, and his achievements would become legion.

King's third administration began inauspiciously in 1935. His government took the Bank of Canada, created as a quasi-governmental agency by Bennett, and made it into a truly national bank that could handle monetary policy. He established a Royal Commission on Dominion-Provincial Relations to investigate the fiscal plight of the provinces, and he edged his government towards a national system of unemployment insurance. There were modest initiatives in housing and, in 1939, the first stimulative deficit budget. Although all important measures, they were far from enough to deal with the problems of the Depression.

Nor was the record stellar on foreign policy. King lent no support to the tepid British and French efforts to rein in Nazi Germany. In his view, Canada had no stake in Eastern Europe, and the tensions at home between French and English Canadians, always raised by the prospect of involvement in a "British" war, demanded that Canada speak softly and with a small stick. But King was no neutralist and he knew what Canada must do if war came. In 1937 he paid a visit to Nazi Germany and met with Adolf Hitler in Berlin. He told the Führer that Canadians would fight if Germany went to war with Britain, and he told a doubtful London exactly what he had said. At the same time, he worked assiduously to cultivate a relationship President Franklin Roosevelt.

King and Roosevelt were not close friends, and the disparity in their nations' power was substantial. Yet they respected each other as political leaders and neighbours. King worried about the gulf between the United States and Britain, and believed with religious fervour that trade made good friends. Within days of taking office in 1935, he was pressing forward trade negotiations with Washington. The resulting agreement, the first since 1854, was a signal that trade relations were going to become closer. Three years later there was a

second agreement, more favourable to Canada. Simultaneously, King and Roosevelt nudged their countries towards
cooperation in defence. Secret staff talks took place, and in
1938 Roosevelt, speaking in Canada, pledged to defend the
country. When war came in 1939, Canada was firmly shel-
tered under the American defence umbrella.

The Second World War was a testing time for King and
Canada. By skilful manoeuvring, King kept the country
united. Conservatives sneered at King as "the American,"
and French-Canadian isolationists pronounced him "ready,
aye ready" anytime Britain called. In fact, King had desperately hoped to stay out of war, but he and his Cabinet,
including justice minister Ernest Lapointe and the Quebec
ministers, had long agreed that Canada had to participate if
Britain went to war. English-Canadian public opinion would
demand nothing less. King's instincts were for a war of
limited liability and, as he declared in March 1939, a war
without conscription for overseas service. When Britain
declared war on Germany on September 3, King delayed
Canada's declaration for a week, time enough for Parliament
to decide the issue for itself—a symbol of Canada's independent status. Soon after, the United Kingdom urged King to
begin negotiations for a British Commonwealth Air Training
Plan. The bargaining was hard, in part because King wanted
London to declare the giant scheme to be Canada's major
contribution to the war—as in fact it would become. For a
time it seemed doubtful that army units would proceed overseas, but public opinion demanded that involvement. Canada
was in the war—reluctantly in Quebec, and with some enthusiasm in English Canada—and still united, thanks to King.

All too soon, King faced attacks from the reluctant and the
enthusiastic. In September, Quebec premier Maurice Duplessis
called a snap election, charging that the federal government

was using the war to centralize power. King's Quebec ministers, promising no conscription, entered the fray and smashed Duplessis. Then, early in 1940, Premier Mitchell Hepburn of Ontario, a Liberal but no supporter of King, charged that the federal government was doing nothing in the war and had his legislature condemn the war effort. King cleverly used this extraordinary action to justify his own election call, catching the opposition completely unready. Again the government pledged itself against conscription and it scored a second huge victory. King was in power with a fresh mandate when, in May and June 1940, Germany forced France to surrender and drove Britain off the continent at Dunkirk.

The war was now a total struggle for survival. If Britain fell, if the Royal Navy came under Hitler's control, North America was open to attack. That didn't happen, but the North Atlantic became a hunting ground for Nazi U-boats and there were sinkings in the St. Lawrence. The situation was grave and King's government abandoned limited liability. There would be a vastly expanded Air Training Plan that eventually produced 131,000 aircrew, a large navy that played an increasingly important role in the North Atlantic convoy war, and a bigger army than in the Great War.

Britain's peril also emboldened the conscriptionists in the country and Cabinet, and King fought a long rearguard action to stave off the inevitable. The first concession came when the National Resources Mobilization Act of June 1940 authorized home defence conscription for thirty days, a term that, over time, stretched to cover the war's duration. In November 1941 a Conservative meeting made Meighen the party leader once again, and the conscription tom-toms began to beat insistently. King countered with a plebiscite that, without mentioning the word *conscription*, asked for release from the government's pledges of 1939–40. The government won, though French Canadians heavily voted *non*. The NRMA was duly amended, but with King's pledge that the change meant "not necessarily conscription, but conscription if necessary," the classic embodiment of Kingian ambiguity. Defence minister J.L. Ralston almost resigned and one Quebec minister did so, but King held the party together until heavy infantry casualties in Italy and Normandy created a reinforcement crisis in the autumn of 1944.

King had almost managed to avoid conscription through brilliant delaying tactics. Now he demonstrated he could move decisively: desperate to keep the country united with the war almost won, King ruthlessly sacked Ralston and appointed General Andrew McNaughton, the former commander of the

First Canadian Army overseas, to take his place. McNaughton tried but failed to persuade home defence conscripts to volunteer for the front and, after an agonizing three weeks, King reversed course and ordered 16,000 conscripts overseas. Quebec reeled, but King prevailed in the House of Commons: "If there is anything to which I have devoted my political life, it is to try to promote unity, harmony and amity between the diverse elements of this country," he said in a great speech. "My friends can desert me, they

National Archives of Canada C-44300

96

can remove their confidence from me, they can withdraw the trust they have placed in my hands, but never shall I deviate from that line of policy . . . I feel that I am in the right, and I know that a time will come when every man will render me full justice on that score." Influenced by his Quebec lieutenant Louis St. Laurent, who calmly accepted the need for conscription, Québécois eventually concluded that King had done his best to hold off compulsory service.

King was similarly successful in his relations with Roosevelt. The defeats on the Continent in 1940 for the first time put Canada's safety in peril, particularly if Britain lost the war. At the president's request, King found himself in the middle, conveying American demands on the future of the British fleet to Winston Churchill. He also found Roosevelt pressing for a defence alliance in August 1940. King agreed: he had no choice, and the alliance let Canada do its utmost to get men and machines overseas without worrying about home defence. The change in imperial masters was fateful. So too was the shift in economic power southward. The war greatly expanded Canadian industry, and required a far greater import of metals, munitions components, and weapons from the United States. By early 1941 Canada had no money to pay its bills to the Americans, and King went to Roosevelt's home at Hyde Park, New York, in April 1941 to plead his case. The result was an agreement that the Americans would buy as much in Canada as Canada was buying in the United States. At a stroke, the Hyde Park Declaration resolved the dollar crisis and allowed Canadian industry to work to capacity. The results, directed by the powerful minister of munitions and supply, C.D. Howe, were impressive. King gave Howe his head, and the results justified the trust.

King never sought any place in Allied strategic decisions, but he wanted Canada's role in key areas to be recognized.

He claimed a special place for Canada in food production, in resources, and in international relief. Aided by a brilliant team in the Department of External Affairs (of which he was the minister), he successfully insisted that Canada sit on the Anglo-American Combined Food Board and the Combined Production and Resources Board, the only middle-sized power to be so recognized.

At the same time, King finally began to implement the 1919 Liberal Party platform. Canadians feared the return of the Depression at war's end, and Cooperative Commonwealth Federation politicians (the forerunner of the New Democratic Party) played skilfully on this concern. In 1940 King had pushed unemployment insurance into law, knowing full well that wartime employment would allow a large insurance fund to be built up for the postwar dislocations. In 1943 the Liberal Party renewed its pledges of social welfare, and in the next two years the government put in place family allowances (this single program cost almost half the total pre-war federal budget), allocated large sums for housing, created a Department of Health and Welfare, and, in the Veterans' Charter, established a superior package of benefits for demobilized servicemen and women. The willingness to use the budget as an economic tool also led the government to create a shelf of large public-works projects to soak up expected postwar unemployment and promise full employment. The contrast with the Borden government's lack of planning for the postwar years could not have been clearer.

The government's war record was superb, and for once King deserved an election sweep, but the 1945 election was still a tough fight. He prevailed by stressing the government's war record, the social welfare policies already in place, the plans for postwar reconstruction, and by denouncing the CCF and Conservatives. King was characteristically in the middle, and he had the support of Quebec. On election day he won 127 seats in a House of 245.

The prime minister now was almost seventy-one years old, and he was perceptibly failing. He had his good days when he

Campaigning, King was willing to sign autographs.

was as sharp as ever, but increasingly his staff found his moods difficult. He had always expected his officials to be available at all hours; now the petulance and inconsideration spiralled out of control. There was no sign of his preparing to step aside, although he indicated his choice of successor when he persuaded Louis St. Laurent to remain in politics in 1945.

The international scene preoccupied King. In September 1945 a Soviet cipher officer, Igor Gouzenko, defected from the embassy in Ottawa with documents proving that the USSR had run spy rings during the war. This affair, quickly communicated to the United States and Britain, demonstrated that public servants could violate their oaths for ideological reasons. It also showed that the Soviet Union, though a wartime ally, remained an implacable foe. The Cold War was imminent, and by 1948 Canada was in secret discussions with London and Washington about the need for a north Atlantic alliance to deter the Soviets.

At the same time, Canada and the United States were discussing free trade, motivated not least by security concerns. King had agreed to the initiation of these discussions, but when a draft treaty was produced in 1948 he developed cold feet. How would he be perceived by history if he tied Canada to its neighbour? That was not an unreasonable response, given the still powerful force of British sentiment in Canada and the attacks that had been levelled for years that he was a continentalist. Summoning his strength, the prime minister scotched the deal. The idea remained dormant for forty years, until Brian Mulroney revived it.

At last it was time to go. In January 1948 King announced that he would retire after a party leadership convention in August. Though he was ostensibly neutral, he clearly gave his support to Louis St. Laurent, who won easily. It was difficult to give up power after twenty-two years, and the handover did not finally take place until November 15, almost a year after the announcement. The old man intended to write his memoirs, based on his astonishing diary and his vast collection of papers, but he never got organized enough to begin. Always lonely, he was left with only a small circle of friends, a few servants, and his beloved dog. Power had kept him alive, and now his health began to break down. He succumbed on July 22, 1950. Crowds turned out to move past his bier in the Parliament Buildings, but there was little emotion. King had never been loved by his people or his colleagues, though many of the latter feared him and some admired him as a leader of skill.

His legacy after twenty-two years in office was a Liberal Party that had become the "government party." The Liberals had held the centre of the road so skilfully and for so long with a politics based on national unity and social welfare that the opposition on both left and right had been disarmed. King had made the Liberal Party the master of reconciliatory politics, and it flourished.

For years after his death, historians were negative about the nation's longest-serving prime minister. King's peculiarities, his attachment to his dead mother and his dogs, his spiritualist yearnings, and his supposed encounters with prostitutes, all recorded in his diaries, fed an unhealthy interest in the bizarre. His shrewd political judgement, his constant attention to French Canada, his great steps forward in Canadian nationhood were, while acknowledged, down-played or distorted by writers and the media. His cautious weighing of options and alternatives—doing nothing by halves that could be done by quarters—was widely viewed as a flaw in his and the Canadian character.

The pendulum of opinion has now swung. King the man remains as difficult to like as ever, but his political leadership skills, his brilliant decisiveness in crises, and his vision of an independent Canada command admiration. No one can rule a nation as disparate as Canada for so long without talents of a high order, and King's place at last is being properly recognized. Just as Norman Lambert observed in 1941, "get off a piece" and he looks better and better.

R. B. Bennett

The Great Depression was a time to try souls, and it sorely tested R.B. Bennett's. The apparent quintessence of a priggish plutocrat, with stiff collar, striped pants, and a dark frockcoat, he hid his generosity and frequently progressive views under a stern and unsympathetic exterior. At times Bennett fought the bruising unemployment and economic collapse of the 1930s with imagination. Like others, he failed; unlike some, he was blackened and branded a failure.

Born in Hopewell Hill, New Brunswick, July 3, 1870; died in Mickleham, Surrey, England, July 26, 1947. Prime minister for five years: August 7, 1930–October 23, 1935

R ichard Bedford Bennett was the best of the candidates who presented themselves for Conservative Party chief in 1927, and it did not hurt that he was very wealthy. He was a reluctant candidate, content with his life as it was and uncertain that he had the stuff of political leadership. Already fifty-seven years old, he was thinking about retirement to England, with a country home and perhaps a seat in the British Parliament. He gave in to those who wanted him to run out of duty and patriotism, he claimed, and promptly declared God on his side in the battle ahead.

Once elected leader, and easily so, he poured his energy and money into the party while disentangling himself from most of his business interests. During his first year on the job, he spent 60 percent of his $250,000 income on the Conservatives. By the time the election of 1930 was called, he had donated at least $500,000, including $100,000 in Quebec. He had also become the secret proprietor, to the tune of a $344,000 investment, of the Regina *Daily Star*, a racy newspaper designed to break the Liberal grip on Saskatchewan.

Bennett came from a New Brunswick family that always had to struggle, and he did not forget "the pit from which I was digged & the long uphill road I had to travel." He seldom mentioned his hard-drinking and light-working father. His model was his mother, Henrietta, who drove upright Methodist values of industry and honesty into her eldest son. She was the mainspring of his life: as he said after her death in 1914, she had been his "teacher, guide, counsellor, companion, friend and above all an impartial and candid critic." Bennett's other powerful and continuing influence was his sister, Mildred, who described herself as the necessary bumper on his car in politics, saving him a lot of damage. Their relationship was unusually intense.

Bennett liked women and could be a sparkling companion on the surface. He wrote to one woman friend from his youth all his life, and he acquired controlling interest in the E.B. Eddy paper empire from another after she died. But he never married. Perhaps, as biographer Peter Waite suggests, he was sexually dysfunctional; perhaps he was just too timid and vulnerable; perhaps business always won out. In his early thirties, solitary and repressed, he declared himself "almost an old man" who would not marry. Besides, wasn't it impossible to find the perfect wife, who had a domestic side yet "such large sympathies and mental qualities as to be able to enter into the ambitions & hopes of her husband whatever they might be"?

Young Dick, as he was called, did not know how to play, only to work. His lifelong friend and fellow-entrepreneur Max Aitken said he was "a young man of too many negatives—no smoking, no drinking, no dancing, no games of chance and . . . no bowling alleys." He began a single-minded professional life at seventeen, as a schoolteacher near his New Brunswick home. He became a very serious principal the next year, lecturing parents and officials with equal ferocity. Saving his money, he travelled to law school at Dalhousie University in Halifax in 1890. He was an excellent student and a political career sprouted: prime minister in the student parliament and a handshake with "our good old man," Sir John A. Macdonald.

In 1897 Bennett migrated to Calgary as legal partner to

Senator James Lougheed. Calgary was his home base for the next thirty years, as he mingled politics, corporate law and a burgeoning business portfolio that included a series of hugely successful deals with Aitken, making them both rich. He served as minister of finance during Meighen's few days in power. In 1926, the third time he was elected to the House of Commons, he was the only Tory returned from the Prairies. In the prosperous, business-loving, self-congratulatory 1920s, he was a genuine star.

By 1930, after three years as leader, Bennett had himself and the Conservatives in shape for an election. Circumstances, in the form of a significant downturn in the economy, favoured change. Contributing a quarter of a million dollars of his own money to the campaign, Bennett took advantage of the moment with whirlwind energy, travelling 14,000 miles, using radio effectively for the first time in a national election, and delivering the thrusting oratory that had given him the nickname "Bonfire Bennett." At his side was Mildred, whose smile was employed as a vote-getting tactic, and William Herridge, a quirky lawyer who devised the most colourful parts of Bennett's forceful appeals to the public.

No one recognized that the Depression had arrived, though Bennett promised action and gave hope in a time of economic uncertainty. Jobs would return, or he would "perish in the attempt." World markets would be "blasted open." Canada would come first, Britain second, and the United States a long way back. As a journalist pointed out, Bennett was an evangelist at heart, "one of those to whom an espoused cause is something to die for." "There is a good time coming," he shouted in Regina. "I came to call the sinners, not the righteous."

Bennett's win was respectable, but not overwhelming. His

careful preparation of the ground in Saskatchewan and Quebec was as important as his leadership style in the final outcome. Those provinces provided the margin of victory, and the twenty-four seats he won in Quebec were extraordinary for a man who had championed compulsory military service during the war and who spoke only halting French.

The new prime minister dived headlong into fourteen- to eighteen-hour days except on Sundays, which were kept sacrosanct. He said he wanted to consult his ministers, but he felt they let him down, so he ended up watching over their details as well as his own. Nor could bureaucrats be trusted to do anything more than "wangle and set aside" their bosses. He did not fire Ottawa's top civil servant, the Liberal O.D. Skelton, and asked his advice frequently, but only to confirm his own opinions. "He is the darndest man to teach anything," said Skelton in 1931. "He always knows something about a subject—I never met a man who knows something about so many things—but he never knows enough & no matter how much I try to enlarge on any particular things—at the end of the interview he will be back to exactly the little & few facts he had at the beginning."

National Archives of Canada C-134104

The popular view that Bennett was a one-man government took root

DICTATORSHIP OUTFITTING COMPANY

Dale / Five Years of R.B. Bennett

SUMMER STYLES, 1935

early. Political cartoonist Arch Dale got under Bennett's skin by depicting Cabinet sessions as the prime minister meeting with himself. "As cold as an Arctic breeze," in one observer's phrase, he became known as an insensitive despot, an idea reinforced by his pledge to grind dissent under "the heel of ruthlessness." Fearing violence and even revolution, he brought out the police and an armoured car to protect him against the twelve representatives of a group of unemployed workers who came to Parliament Hill to read a petition. "Once in the saddle, swift the whip he cracks. / The Mounties spring like thistles in his tracks," wrote poet F.R. Scott. Another of Dale's caricatures showed the prime minister approvingly sizing up the uniforms of Stalin, Hitler, and Mussolini at the Dictatorship Outfitting Company.

Increasingly, Bennett was a figure of fun and derision. He was coming to personify the cruel hardship of the Depression: "Bennett buggies" were horse-drawn cars; "Bennett brew" was a pale coffee made with grain; "Bennett barn-yards" were abandoned farms; and "Bennett boroughs" were shanty towns.

The private Bennett was an old softie. He raged at Skelton, but touched him as well with acts of kindness—putting the prime minister's chauffeur and car at the family's disposal; telling Skelton to go off for an evening with his wife rather than stay at work; writing him letters in the warmest terms. Such treatment from Mackenzie King would have been unimaginable. To Canadians who sent him accounts of their personal hardship, he frequently returned a gift of cash from his own hefty wallet.

As time went on, Bennett was forced to delegate more to Skelton and a few others, in part because of frequent health problems. He was ill with one ailment or another every year and had a major heart attack in 1935. Urged to let up on his punishing schedule, he simply replied that if "he was to go, he'd go." Men's whole lives turned on slight twists of chance. There was nothing to do but work hard and accept what fate had to offer. When Mildred married Bill Herridge in 1931, just after Bennett named him Canada's representative in Washington, he lost his one constant companion. He carried on a passionate love affair with a stylish widow named Hazel Colville soon afterwards, and it broke his heart when they could not get through their differences.

Bennett, who was his own finance minister at the beginning of his administration, applied the conventional tools to the economy. He heaped on the tariffs, passed a massive $20 million relief package for the unemployed, and went off to England to encourage closer trading ties with Britain. Nothing worked. Six months after the election he admitted that Canada was in a severe economic depression. The explanation, in his view, lay in laziness, extravagance, speculation, and dishonesty. What Canadians needed was a dose of religion and sweat. Labour camps for the single unemployed, administered by the army, were one of Bennett's cures for hard times. They regularly housed up to 20,000 men, but did nothing to enhance his popularity.

The 1932 Commonwealth economic conference in Ottawa put the prime minister on display at his worst. It was his great dream to assemble the countries of the old British Empire into a trading juggernaut, but he enraged the other delegates with his brusqueness, poor preparation, and changeability. One member of the British delegation was convinced that the Canadian was tapping their telephones, while another complained that he simply lied and cried in equal measure. The meeting resulted in a series of trade accords, the Ottawa Agreements, but also in more bad blood and recrimination than any other Commonwealth meeting in history. When it came right down to it, Bennett, for all his professed pro-British fervour, was as fierce a Canadian nationalist as Mackenzie King, and much less of a diplomat about it.

Trying to explain Bennett's strange behaviour, the secretary to the governor general wrote that "aggression is the only method of negotiation that he knows . . . One who has known Bennett for many years is reported to have said of him, 'R.B. is partially educated, but wholly uncivilised.' With this somewhat primitive habit of mind go several other primitive characteristics; an almost savage sensitiveness to ridicule, small vanities, a child-like impatience of obstacles, an equally child-like appreciation of sympathy and small acts of friendliness—traits that are, perhaps, not . . . infrequently found with first-rate intellectual capacity, which he certainly has." An opposition politician was even less charitable: Bennett had the manners of a Chicago policeman and the temperament of a Hollywood actor.

By 1934 the prime minister wanted to retire, but he could not. He had a full-scale revolt on his hands, courtesy of his trade minister, Harry Stevens, who had become a public champion of small business, labour, and consumers against the big interests. The T. Eaton Company, he claimed, paid its forty directors around $35,000 each and its employees less than $1,000 on average. Stevens resigned late in the year and in 1935 formed his own faction, the Reconstruction Party. Even before that, the two men were competitors to prove who cared the most about the downtrodden—"the masses and the asses," in a cynic's jest. "If that skunk is to be skinned," Bennett told a reporter of Stevens, "I suppose I'll have to do the job."

Bennett's response was his "New Deal," a conscious imitation (right down to the hopeful name) of United States president Franklin Roosevelt's declaration of war against the Depression through state intervention in the economy. In a series of live radio broadcasts early in 1935, the prime minister discussed a dramatic expansion of the Canadian government's powers to regulate the economy. "The old order is gone. It will not return," he enthused in words written for him by Bill Herridge, who had been watching the American New Deal from his perch in Washington and urged the idea on his brother-in-law. "I nail the flag of progress to the masthead," Bennett pledged. "I summon the power of the State to its support." He denounced "corporations without souls." They would not be allowed to continue their "immemorial right of exploitation."

This was not socialism, although some Conservative Cabinet ministers feared it was. No one could blame them. A desperate Bennett had taken this path on his own, without consulting any of his Cabinet. He was not out to slay capitalism, but to tame it, so it "will be your servant and not your master." Decisive federal government action would manage the economy, big government curbing big business and big labour. The New Deal, Bennett and Herridge hoped, would get the people's attention, demonstrating that the government was on their side and had been all along.

Bennett and his beloved sister Mildred made a powerful campaign team.

From his early political days, Bennett had never shared the hatred of government associated with members of the business class. He came to respect the public service, or parts of it, and established major national institutions such as the Canadian Broadcasting Corporation and the Bank of Canada. He was a "Red Tory," one political expert judged, a Conservative with a social conscience. "An authentic radical," insists historian Waite. The "unredeemed capitalist, with dollar signs on his striped trousers and black coat. His appearance was the greatest illusion of them all."

But little came of the New Deal. It briefly gave Bennett the desired initiative, but he was outmanoeuvred by the Liberals in the House of Commons, hounded by opposition from within, and felled by his bad heart. With the prime minister supervising every detail, legislation was improvised on unemployment insurance and minimum hours and wages, but the performance fell far short of the promise. "I fear our big, beautiful reform child is dead," Herridge lamented as the Bennett reform program flopped. Later on, most of the New Deal legislation was thrown out by the courts for having exceeded the authority of the federal government.

There was no avoiding an election, which was required every five years, and Bennett's time was up. One last vote-getting possibility remained: a trade agreement with the United States. The Americans, remembering his high tariffs and tough nationalist talk all too well, had difficulty believing he was sincere and stable. They could wait until a more friendly government came to power.

Mildred rushed home to help him campaign: "I love Dick so much that often I long to see him defeated but . . . we must put Canada first," she said. Without a real reform package or a trade pact to hawk, Bennett could only declare that the economy had improved—fewer than 500,000 Canadians were now unemployed, by his calculation—and emphasize that it was either law and order or the rule of the rabble. He worked very hard for his re-election, bouncing back from his heart attack, talking to large if sometimes heckling groups, and dominating with sheer will. "Canada needs a fighter," the Conservatives cried. "Vote for Bennett." The Liberals replied that it was "King or Chaos." They coasted to power on a reminder that the prime minister had not delivered on his original 1930 promise of jobs and markets. Bennett was consigned to three unhappy years as leader of the opposition.

R.B. could still control his party easily enough, but that was a big part of the problem. There was no one else among

Conservatives to look up to, or even to despise. He was all Canadians could see. Lacking Laurier's sunny ways or King's shrewd understanding of the political art of delegating responsibility and blame, Bennett utterly failed as a leader. Everyone was alienated by the end—Cabinet, caucus, party, voter, and foreigner. He neglected the Tory organization he had built up so carefully before 1930 and squandered the beachhead he had established in Quebec, the only Conservative breakthrough between the conscription election of 1917 and John Diefenbaker's romp in 1958. By 1935 he was carrying out a full-throated argument with railways minister Robert Manion in the House of Commons. Only one in three electors voted for Bennett in 1935.

He left the leadership nursing considerable grievances, under-appreciated in his party and rejected by Canadians. He spoke of the ingratitude of public life: "I am not unaware of my own limitations. I have made many mistakes, but I have served this country as disinterestedly as any man who ever occupied public office, and I have never expected more than loyalty . . . That I did not receive it may perhaps be a criticism of myself."

In the same year that Bennett left politics, Mildred died before reaching her fiftieth birthday. Bennett moved to England immediately, returning to Canada only once after that. He got his English country manor, taking up residence beside Max Aitken, now Lord Beaverbrook. In 1941 he entered the House of Lords as Viscount Bennett of Mickleham, Calgary, and Hopewell. His death, of a final heart seizure in the bathtub of his grand master bedroom, was greeted by comfortable postwar Canada with indifference. He was as much a relic of the past as the Depression itself.

Louis St. Laurent

Highly intelligent, serene, fluently bilingual, Louis St. Laurent made governing Canada look easy. He presided over a powerful government that built huge national projects such as the St. Lawrence Seaway and rearmed the country for the Cold War. He did it all with an avuncular style that inspired trust—until the public's distaste for what it came to see as Liberal arrogance destroyed him.

Born in Compton, Quebec, February 1, 1882; died in Quebec City, Quebec, July 25, 1973. Prime minister for nine years: November 15, 1948–June 21, 1957

The eldest son of a francophone father and an Irish-Canadian mother, Louis St. Laurent grew up completely and naturally bilingual in the Eastern Townships of Quebec. His father was a small-town storekeeper with an active interest in the Liberal Party. The highlight of the son's youth was to see the great Sir Wilfrid Laurier shake his father's hand and call him by name. His own commitment to Liberalism was sealed forever.

St. Laurent's education in backwoods Compton was spotty, but the teacher in the small Catholic school he attended recognized his intelligence. With her encouragement, he went to the classical college in nearby Sherbrooke, where he led his class, and then to law school at Université Laval, where in 1905 he again placed first. He struggled to get established in the law in Quebec City, and by 1908 had begun to make his mark and to represent important clients, not least the provincial government. He had also married Jeanne Renault and soon had a family.

St. Laurent was a French Canadian of his era, and his attitudes reflected those of the society in which he moved and lived. Catholicism was the rock on which he stood, family was the key, and hard work was the route to success. He was no Bourassa *nationaliste*—his Liberalism remained solid—and he was not attracted by the paranoid mutterings of *Le Devoir*. Even so, he had serious doubts about Canada's involvement in the Great War, and he opposed the Borden

115

government's imposition of conscription in 1917. When the government sent troops from Toronto to Quebec City to restore order after anti-conscription rioting broke out in the spring of 1918, St. Laurent was outraged.

He was a lawyer, first and foremost, and politics held little attraction for him. He joined the Canadian Bar Association at its founding, and was soon one of the leading lights of the profession. He represented innumerable clients before the Supreme Court and, in an era when the Judicial Committee of the Privy Council was the highest court of appeal in the British Empire, he regularly crossed the Atlantic to plead cases before it. (As prime minister, he would end appeals to the Judicial Committee, making the Supreme Court the nation's highest appelate tribunal.) A corporate law specialist, he was a wealthy man by the time the Great Depression fell on Canada in the 1930s.

When the Mackenzie King government appointed a Royal Commission on Dominion-Provincial Relations in 1937, St. Laurent was named one of its legal advisers. This position gave him the chance to travel across Canada with the commissioners, and he found himself shaken at the devastation wrought by dust, grasshoppers, and crop failures. The Prairies lay in ruins, their recovery hampered by a constitution that gave them powers but no funds. Moved emotionally, changed intellectually, St. Laurent actively supported the commission's recommendations that subsidies henceforth flow from a strong central government to the provinces.

The implementation of the commission's recommendations was short-circuited by the Second World War. Ernest Lapointe, the longtime Quebec lieutenant to Mackenzie King, manoeuvred carefully to bring Quebec willingly into the war in September 1939 and to keep the province's support solid for the Liberal government. But Lapointe died in November

1941 and King quickly turned to the still little-known Quebec lawyer to become his replacement as justice minister.

The issue of the day was whether Canada should fight the war with conscription, an idea advanced by Arthur Meighen, the recently reincarnated Conservative leader, and by some anglophone Cabinet ministers. The Cabinet was wrestling with the issue, its hands largely tied by King's and Lapointe's promises during the Quebec election of 1939 and the federal election of March 1940 that there would be no conscription for overseas service. Though the war was going badly, the

St. Laurent and King at the Liberal leadership convention, 1948.

reluctance to break the government's promises remained strong. St. Laurent understood the evils of Naziism, however, and he backed the prime minister in his plan for a plebiscite to release the government from its pledges against conscription.

This did not mean compulsory service now, he told the electors in Lapointe's old riding of Quebec East, where he was running in a by-election; for his part, he was prepared to trust Mackenzie King's judgement on whether conscription ever need be implemented. To hear a Quebec politician say something other than "no conscription" was a sharp break from the province's isolationist and anti-imperial tradition. It was also an indication that St. Laurent already carried an effortless moral authority that made Quebecers trust him.

The new minister soon became King's strong right arm, the unquestioned Quebec lieutenant. His mind was crystal clear on issues, his judgement sound, his genuine devotion to the "partnership of the two historic races" obvious. He could be tough in using the powers of the state—it was St. Laurent who authorized the suspension of habeas corpus when Igor Gouzenko's defection revealed the existence of Soviet spy rings in Canada at war's end and suspects were incarcerated without access to legal counsel—and he understood the importance of winning the war. In late 1944, when infantry reinforcements for the troops fighting in Europe could be found only among the home defence conscripts serving in Canada, St. Laurent supported the prime minister in sending conscripts overseas. By that action, he all but guaranteed King's survival as leader—and his own eventual ascension to the prime ministership. So respected had he become in Quebec that his pro-conscription stance, while it was not welcomed, was understood and largely accepted. Canadians have not generally admired the character of their leaders, and St. Laurent stands out because he was genuinely respected. This, combined with his financial security, gave him unusual freedom to manoeuvre, to take positions, and to act without fear of the consequences.

Whatever his standing, St. Laurent had no intention of

remaining in politics at war's end. He had joined the government as a wartime duty. But King prevailed on him to stay and took him to San Francisco for the founding conference of the United Nations in 1945; the next year, King made St. Laurent acting prime minister when he attended the Paris Peace Conference. Retirement was still on St. Laurent's mind, but when the prime minister offered him the post of secretary of state for external affairs, the first time that ministry would be held by anyone other than a prime minister, St. Laurent relented and remained. The die was now cast.

Times were difficult, with the postwar world in ruins, the United States largely isolationist, and the Soviet Union spreading its control over Eastern Europe and its tentacles throughout France and Italy. St. Laurent, deeply religious, feared godless communism and, working with his undersecretary, Lester Pearson, he played a critical role in mobilizing the West to resist Marxism. One speech in 1947 was the first to hint at an alliance of North Atlantic nations if the United Nations could not provide the collective security it promised—and by the next year, as Czechoslovakia was swallowed whole by the Soviets, it was clear that it could not. St. Laurent and Pearson led Canada into the North Atlantic Treaty Organization in April 1949, a major shift in the nation's role, a sign of new national confidence, and yet another indication of St. Laurent's willingness to break with the tenets of Quebec isolationism. There was some opposition in Quebec to this direction, but St. Laurent dealt with it head on, telling Québécois that the communists had jailed prelates all over Eastern Europe. In one speech in St.-Jean-sur-Richelieu, he turned to an archbishop and said he did not want to see that happen to him.

By then St. Laurent was Canada's twelfth prime minister, and Pearson his foreign minister. Mackenzie King had finally stepped down in the autumn of 1948, and the Quebecer had handily won the Liberal leadership on the first ballot. By doing so, he became Canada's second French-Canadian prime minister, and he firmly established the principle of alternating French- and English-speaking leaders of the Liberal Party.

"Uncle Louis."

His first task was to win an election in his own right, and in the late spring of 1949, fresh from the triumph of bringing Newfoundland into Confederation and completing Canada "from sea to sea," St. Laurent went to the polls. His main opponent was the Progressive Conservative leader, George Drew, a former Ontario premier. Drew was tall, grave, and a bit of a stuffed shirt; St. Laurent was tall, grave, and gracious, kissing babies, patting children on the head, shaking hands, and generally charming everyone he met. "Uncle Louis will be tough to beat," one reporter observed after a day of campaigning, and the nickname stuck. Campaigning with few promises other than to continue Canada's postwar prosperity, Uncle Louis won a huge majority, taking 192 of the 262 seats in the House of Commons.

In power, St. Laurent was as businesslike and straightforward, hard-working and direct as R.B. Bennett, though he had infinitely more public appeal than the hated Depression leader. He studied the dossiers that came before him, checking the facts and mastering their contents, and knew as much about the details of the issues as the minister responsible. If

120

they were competent, if they knew their facts, the ministers had as much room as they wanted; if not, they were tightly controlled or replaced. For his part, decisions almost always flowed logically from the facts of the case, and he had little or no trouble in making up his mind with promptness. All he lacked was deviousness, the key trait of most successful prime ministers. Somehow, this straightforward man did not seem to require it to govern successfully.

St. Laurent struck up good relations with American presidents Truman and Eisenhower and, as one who feared Soviet expansionism and communism, he cooperated with them in NATO and in North American defence. At the outbreak of the Korean War in June 1950, he presided over Canada's greatest peacetime military buildup, sending an infantry brigade group to Korea and another to Western Europe—along with an air division of fighter aircraft. This defence buildup was not Mackenzie King's style of leadership, nor was it traditional Quebec isolationism. Instead, this was Canada's first ever peacetime commitment of troops overseas. St. Laurent, a man born in the reign of Queen Victoria and in an era of simpler issues, was a positive Canadian, leading the nation into a new and dangerous world with a sure sense of where he wanted to go.

The economy boomed under the stimulus of rearmament, and C.D. Howe, St. Laurent's right-hand man and the "minister of everything," exercised a firm hand on the financial levers. The nation wanted great projects—a Trans-Canada Highway System, a St. Lawrence Seaway—and the Liberals delivered, becoming what their leader called "a building government." The people wanted equalization payments designed to make the minimum standard of living in one province the same as in any other, and St. Laurent came through. They wanted universal old age pensions, and they received them. They wanted Canadian culture to flourish, and St. Laurent's government established the Canada Council to foster the arts and help the universities. And still the budgets were balanced almost every year.

Like every French-speaking prime minister before or since, St. Laurent had special difficulties with Quebec. Premier Maurice Duplessis of Quebec played the provincial-rights card at every opportunity. He was quick to accuse St. Laurent of selling out French-Canadian rights when he offered money to the provincial governments in areas that were Quebec's under the constitution. For his part, the prime minister considered that Quebec was a province like the others and gave little ground to the premier. To St. Laurent, "the central power does not derive its existence and authority from the provinces and it does not need to go back to the provinces in order to say what Canada shall be in the future." The Compact Theory so beloved of Quebec premiers, the idea that the provinces had created the federal government and were equal to it, had little truth in it for the prime minister. St. Laurent dealt with Duplessis fairly, always trying to find the workable compromise that could satisfy everyone. He failed, but he mitigated the premier's unhappiness sufficiently that the Liberals never lost the support of Quebec's voters. Regrettably, St. Laurent, bilingual from the day he started talking, failed to do much to ameliorate the inability or unwillingness of the federal government and its agencies to deal—in French—with Quebecers. The prime minister did not believe in special concessions.

For the first seven or so years in power, the complaints scarcely mattered. Even George Drew, the opposition leader, fell under St. Laurent's spell, disarmed by his courtliness and consideration and by invitations to dinner at the prime minister's house on Sussex Drive. Certainly the voters were charmed, returning the Liberals with another big majority in 1953, and few expected anything else when the next election rolled around.

Then, somehow, it all started to go wrong. Nationalists complained that the Americans were buying up Canadian companies and resources and that the Pentagon controlled Canadian defence policy. American economic expansionism and hunger for national resources had fed a drive northward. Prosperity followed the American dollars, but Canadians began to worry that they were simultaneously tied to Wall Street and the Pentagon. At the same time, political scientists suggested that the Liberals had been in power so long that the civil service had become the handmaiden of government policy. The media, concerned with the powers that C.D. Howe had collected, fretted about the top-down control

National Archives of Canada C-27108

exercised by "the government party." St. Laurent could scarcely understand these complaints. Did Canadians want the jobs and economic progress that US investment brought, or would they prefer to leave their raw materials in the ground? Did they want the military security provided by the alliance with the United States, or would they prefer to be alone in a hard world? Did they prefer ill-thought-out policies or the best ideas produced by the best government advisers? The choices seemed clear to him—investment from wherever it could be secured, defence cooperation with the Americans, and a public service that worked hand-in-glove with the government and its ministers.

By the mid-1950s, St. Laurent was in his middle seventies and his avuncular style was beginning to wear thin with Canadians. All that was needed was one big blowup to shake the throne, and in 1956 two crises came. The first issue arose over a natural gas pipeline designed to bring Alberta gas to Ontario and Quebec markets. This huge project was clearly in the national interest, but the government presented the issue to Parliament and the public in a clumsy fashion. Opposition members seized on the way Howe had negotiated the deal with an American-led consortium. It was another sellout to the Yankees, they charged, and the media picked up the issue. When Howe compounded matters by stonewalling in Parliament and imposing closure on the debate, the Conservatives and the CCF denounced Liberal arrogance. For the first time, people began to believe the charges. The pipeline went through, but the government was badly wounded.

The Suez Crisis of October and November 1956 saw Britain and France invade Egypt in cooperation with Israel to recapture control of the Suez Canal, crucial to Anglo-French commerce and prestige. London saw Egypt's President Nasser as a minor-league Hitler; France was worried about anti-colonialism in its empire; and the Israelis feared that the Arabs might unite against them. For Canada, what mattered was that the British had lied privately to St. Laurent and publicly to the world about their intentions, and the prime minister was justly outraged. Although he encouraged Pearson to save London's bacon by creating a United Nations Emergency Force, he exploded in Parliament, telling the House that the era of the supermen of Europe was over. That incident did not sit well with British loyalists in the Progressive Conservative Party and the media, who denounced the Liberals for being Washington's choreboy. In December, when the Tories replaced Drew with John Diefenbaker, a Prairie populist and a mesmerizing orator, the seeds of St. Laurent's downfall were well and truly planted.

Even so, the election of 1957 was expected to be another Grit victory. Diefenbaker was largely unknown in the country, and the government seemed much too strong to be ejected. So certain did a Liberal victory appear that *Maclean's*, caught between deadlines, gambled and went to press with an editorial that Canadians had re-elected the most powerful government in the Western world. In fact, in a stunning upset, the electorate had given Diefenbaker the most seats, though not a majority. Some Liberals urged St. Laurent to emulate Mackenzie King in 1925 and hang on to power, but the gentlemanly and correct prime minister refused and handed the reins to the Conservatives. It was a stunning turn of events that left St. Laurent profoundly, perhaps clinically, depressed.

The Liberal leadership soon passed to Pearson, and St. Laurent returned to his home on Grande Allée in Quebec City. A great and gentle man, he lived a long time in retirement and resumed the law practice he had abandoned in 1941. He was out of politics for good.

Almost always underestimated then and later, St. Laurent's record had verged on the brilliant. With his lucid mind, he had directed the government sagely through a period of economic boom and global unrest. Not for St. Laurent the hanging back that characterized his predecessor's foreign policy. He wanted to see Canada play its full part in the world. St. Laurent's prime ministership marked the golden age of Canadian foreign policy, the time when Canadian diplomats brought ideas and power to the table. He was master of his Cabinet and the shaper of its policies—which almost literally put two chickens in every Canadian's pot— and finally eliminated the memory of the Depression years. His government sometimes may have acted in a paternalistic, arrogant fashion, certain it knew best, but St. Laurent himself never assumed any airs. He was quiet competence personified. As his principal aide Jack Pickersgill later noted dryly, St. Laurent had made governing Canada look so easy that the people thought anyone could do it—and thus they elected John Diefenbaker.

John Diefenbaker

"I have a vision," he cried, and Canadians hearkened to him. John Diefenbaker galvanized political life with his fervour and, for a time, that was enough, as he won the largest majority so far recorded. But he showed little competence in governing and, except in the West from which he sprang, Canadians turned violently against him.

Born in Neustadt, Ontario, September 18, 1895; died in Ottawa, August 16, 1979. Prime minister for six years: June 21, 1957–April 22, 1963

"They had always opposed me," John Diefenbaker said many times, and "they" were an infinitely expandable list that included Liberals and CCFers, central Canadians, French Canadians, the big interests, and many individuals and groups in the Progressive Conservative Party. While it is a truism that paranoid personalities have enemies, Diefenbaker's band of bitter foes was often self-created and cherished. Certainly no Canadian leader was as difficult a personality; no prime minister in our history raised himself up so quickly or brought himself down so totally.

Born in Ontario, raised in Saskatchewan, Diefenbaker, like King and Bennett, grew up in a home where his mother was the stronger personality. His father was a failed homesteader and public servant who never made much of a success of his life, but young John was a bright student with a gift for words. His mother's praise was everything. He went to university in Saskatoon and, during the First World War, found that his Germanic surname made him the victim of discrimination and the slurs of his fellow students. Perhaps that helped drive him to enlist and to go overseas as a junior officer. His military career was undistinguished, however, and the army invalided him out before he got to France. At least Diefenbaker, unlike so many other young men who went off to war, returned in one piece.

Diefenbaker's subsequent career was defined by the law. He graduated from law school and in 1919 hung out his shingle in Wakaw, Saskatchewan. In that tiny town, he took every case that came his way, from searching property titles to defending murderers, and he became well known for his advocacy. Naturally that turned him to politics, and from the mid-1920s onwards Diefenbaker began running for everything in sight—for Parliament, the legislature, and, after he moved to Prince Albert, the city council. Year after year, election after election, he failed to win the voters' support. Not until 1940, running for the Tories in an election that Mackenzie King's Liberals swept, did Diefenbaker secure a narrow victory in the Lake Centre constituency. His wife, Edna, attractive and outgoing, had campaigned hard for him, and Diefenbaker's own oratory, its almost biblical cadences already well developed, mesmerized the electorate.

In Ottawa, he was a hectoring presence on the Tory benches, and a harsh critic of the government's war record, its "coddling" of French Canada, and its abuses of human rights. In 1948 he ran for the party leadership but lost easily to George Drew, the Ontario premier. Still, he continued to travel the country on the chicken-and-peas circuit, speaking to any group that would have him, presenting his spare frame, aquiline features, and grey, marcelled hair to potential voters. He cultivated journalists, relaxing with them at day's end, regaling them with his memorable impressions of Liberal front-benchers, and laughing at their jokes. After his wife's death in 1951, Diefenbaker met an old school friend, Olive Palmer, and married her in 1953. She reinforced his ambitions with her own. When Drew stepped down in 1956, Diefenbaker was ready, this time winning the leadership easily.

Diefenbaker exploited the Liberal government's weaknesses brilliantly in the election of 1957 as he campaigned against "minister of everything" C.D. Howe's arrogant assumptions that Parliament was the government's plaything, that Canadians wanted to be closely allied with the Americans, and that everyone had it good in mid-1950s Canada. He was overtly nationalist: "My theme is One Country—One Policy," he told a Maritimes audience. "Our policy embraces the whole of Canada . . . with a positive message of hope and progress." "It's Time for a Diefenbaker Government," the party ads shouted, calling for a "New National Policy."

But no one expected victory. There were few Tory votes in Quebec (and he spoke only the most rudimentary French), so Diefenbaker's campaign focused on the English-Canadian seats that could be won. Win he did, to the astonishment of the media, which had predicted another Liberal triumph. Though he failed to secure a majority, Diefenbaker had the most seats, and St. Laurent graciously turned power over to him. The new prime minister, more than slightly stunned by his success, told the governor general that he could "hardly believe this has happened."

The first term—less than a year long—was a triumph. The Chief, as he now became known to everyone, raised old age pensions and pensions for the blind and disabled. He put a winter works program in place, gave more money to the provinces, and cut taxes. He named Ellen Fairclough to the Cabinet, the first woman to sit at the apex of power. And when the Liberal leader, Lester Pearson, foolishly used the occasion of his first speech in Parliament as leader of the opposition to call on Diefenbaker to give power back to the Liberals, who, he said, knew how to run a government, the Chief pounced and got a snap dissolution from the governor general. In the 1958 election campaign Diefenbaker jeered mercilessly at the Liberals. In brilliant, stirring oratory he told Canadians of his "vision" for the future, a Canada that opened itself to the great North, a nation moved by "Faith in Canada's Future, Faith in Her Destiny." He won the largest majority in

Canadian history to that point, sweeping every region of Canada, including Quebec, and taking 208 of 265 seats. The Tories' chance to hold power for a generation seemed in the party's hands.

Too soon, everything started to go wrong. The Conservative ministers mistrusted their civil service advisers—Liberals all, they seemed to believe. Diefenbaker himself was terribly suspicious of the External Affairs bureaucrats—"Pearsonalities," he sneered, all friends of the Liberal leader. The economy, which had boomed ever since the war, began to slow down and unemployment rose, causing union unrest and political fallout. The British deeply resented Diefenbaker's efforts to prevent them from joining the European Common Market, and they were far from pleased with the Canadian leader's successful campaign to throw South Africa out of the Commonwealth because of its apartheid policies. James Coyne, the governor of the Bank of Canada, upset the

National Archives of Canada PA–112659

government with his monetary policy, and the Cabinet messily forced him to resign. Against such a string of problems, even the success of steering Diefenbaker's cherished Bill of Rights into law paled. The bill was largely toothless, but it stood for two decades as a statement of the national commitment to equality.

Washington had grown used to working with cooperative Liberals during the Eisenhower administration of the 1950s.

Diefenbaker and the Bill of Rights, his proudest accomplishment.

The Pentagon had rejoiced when Diefenbaker signed the North American Air Defence Agreement (NORAD), joining the air defences of the two nations under a single command in his first days in power. Unlike Canadians, the US military was not upset when Diefenbaker cancelled the Avro Arrow, an expensive high-performance fighter-interceptor, because Canada could not afford to pay the development costs. And they were positively delighted when he agreed to accept US-supplied nuclear weapons, including Bomarc surface-to-air missiles, to defend North America against Soviet bombers. But Diefenbaker stalled on the implementation of NORAD and the installation of the nuclear missiles, and he sold huge quantities of wheat to Communist China. Washington, which favoured as little trade as possible with a Cold War adversary, was furious.

The Chief became even more arrogant than the Liberals he had driven from power, but simultaneously hesitant and unsure. He never wholly trusted his senior Cabinet ministers who had run against him in 1956 or opposed him at some point in the past. "They" were disloyal. He could never figure out what to do with the horde of MPs the voters had given him in 1958, and he was too often short-tempered in Parliament. He believed in his own judgement and that of his few cronies, but all too often he had terrible trouble making decisions. The Cabinet debated issues endlessly as Diefenbaker sought consensus on issues such as nuclear weapons where there was none. Even subjects such as the confirmation of death sentences on murderers absorbed endless hours of Cabinet time. His government wallowed while the Liberals rebuilt.

In the 1962 election, Diefenbaker just scraped by with a minority government, his support strong only on the Prairies. In four years he had fallen from the heights, and now he clung to office. He was depressed, in pain from a broken ankle, and he told his ministers, "I didn't ask for this job, and I don't want it. If I'm no longer wanted, I'll go." Speculators staged a run on the dollar after the election, and there were disputes in the Cabinet, the caucus, and the Conservative Party over putting the nuclear warheads on the weapons the government had secured when it scrapped the Arrow. Diefenbaker had bought the weapons to support Canada's role in NATO and NORAD, but he persuaded himself that Canadians didn't want them and, because the Americans did, that his government should delay any decision on taking the weapons. The defence and external affairs ministers and their departments were at odds—critics jeered that on Mondays and Wednesdays the prime minister favoured accepting the warheads and on Tuesdays and Thursdays he opposed them.

By January 1963, after the retiring supreme commander of NATO's European forces complained in Ottawa that the government had not lived up to its defence commitments, the Cabinet fell apart. Ministers resigned, Parliament voted non-confidence, and an attempted political coup within the Cabinet and caucus failed narrowly. The Chief was finished, or so it seemed, and there were widespread rumours that he was suffering from Parkinson's Disease or, even worse, had gone mad.

Instead, to everyone's total surprise, not least Pearson's Liberals, Diefenbaker fought a magnificent election campaign. Travelling by train from small town to small town, he talked to his people, and the voters concluded he cared enough to come. They listened when the Chief charged that the Liberals were in Washington's pocket, while he was a Canadian first and foremost. That was why President John F. Kennedy wanted him out of power and Pearson in. The nuclear weapons were useless, he claimed, designed only to divert Soviet missiles to Canada (a curious argument, considering that he had bought the weapons). "They"—the interests, the media, the big cities, the Americans—were against him while only the little people loved him. It was almost true, but outside the West there were too few of the small-town voters left to keep Dief in office. Even so, he won more seats than anyone had forecast a month before the election. His undoubted triumph denied the Liberals a majority and was one of the greatest turnarounds in Canada's political history. The nationalist and anti-American card had worked for Borden in 1911, and Diefenbaker almost made it work for him a half-century later.

For the next four years, Diefenbaker tormented the Pearson government. He charged that the Liberals were corrupt, and he and his MPs unearthed scandal after scandal, most involving Quebec MPs. He opposed Pearson's new maple-leaf flag, blatantly painting it as a concession to Quebec and as the abandonment of Canada's British heritage. In Question Period, day after day, Diefenbaker slammed the prime minister and the government, his finger pointing accusingly, his jowls quivering with indignation, feigned or genuine. For its part, the Pearson government stumbled, and the 1965 election, confidently called to secure a majority for the Liberals, once again produced a minority. It was another Diefenbaker victory, almost the equal of 1963.

The opposition to the Chief within his own party was swelling. Diefenbaker represented the old Canada, the nation of farms and small towns, the Anglo-Canada that did not understand the aspirations of Quebec. The new Canada was urban and bicultural, the media insisted, and Diefenbaker had to be

National Archives of Canada PA–145061

Defeated but defiant, Diefenbaker tried in vain to rally the party to his side in 1966.

pushed to step down. He was outraged at the backbiting: "No leader can go forward," he said in 1966, "when he has to turn around to see who is trying to trip him from behind." Led by Progressive Conservative Party president Dalton Camp, party insiders finally forced a vote on Diefenbaker's leadership, and the Chief, fighting to the end, was out. There was a certain sadness in his comment: "There is nothing as lonely as the leadership of a national party. If things go right, others take the credit. If things go wrong, the leader takes it—excoriated, condemned." Although Diefenbaker made a half-hearted run for the leadership at the 1967 convention that chose Nova Scotia premier Robert Stanfield, he came a weak fifth, his supporters a tiny band from his Prairie bastion. It was a new Progressive Conservative Party now.

The old man stayed in Parliament for another dozen years, his barbs directed at his successors as much as at the Liberal government. Diefenbaker could always be counted on to give the media a pithy comment on any subject: Flora MacDonald, a party worker who had opposed him and subsequently won election to the House of Commons, Dief said, was the finest woman to walk the streets of Kingston since John A.'s day. Soon the politician that many had hated somehow transformed himself into an icon, a national treasure, a loveable, old curmudgeon cherished for his wit and his passionate espousal of causes. His three volumes of memoirs, arguably the most mendacious ever written by a Canadian politician, burnished his own image and refought all the old battles with only one victor.

When he died in 1979 and his body was carried to Saskatoon by train, Canadians of all stripes were deeply moved. The man from the Prairies at last had gone home for good. Yet the record remained, one of deliberate divisiveness, scandalmongering, and mistrust.

Lester B. Pearson

The perennial Canadian boy scout, L.B. Pearson was a Nobel Prize–winning diplomat uncomfortable with the barnstorming, barracking, and loud public appeals of politics. His five years as prime minister were marred by government disorganization, Cabinet leaks, accusations of scandal, and the worst political partisanship Canadians had seen in half a century. Yet Pearson's legislative record was one of substantial achievement, from the flag to Medicare, and much of modern Canada bears his stamp.

Born in Newtonbrook, Ontario, April 23, 1897; died in Ottawa, December 27, 1972. Prime minister for five years: April 22, 1963–April 20, 1968

Everyone who knew him remarked on it: the prime minister was a mystery. L.B. Pearson was the most gregarious of men, quick to lighten serious moments with self-deprecating humour and breaking frequently into an irresistible smile. But he was very hard to penetrate, "a deep one whose secret self very few, if any, can know." His son, Geoffrey, remembered his "distaste for confrontation, an emotional distance which my sister and I came to know as children and to exploit at times." Journalist Robert Fulford described Pearson's mirror-like quality, so that colleagues and acquaintances simply got themselves and their ideas reflected back at them. Naturally enough, they liked what they saw. He listened intently, seeming to prefer that to talking. Nodding his agreement, he never failed to send people away convinced that he agreed with them. Meanwhile, he had revealed nothing.

Lester Bowles Pearson grew up as the twentieth century began to unfold. He believed that the British Empire and the Methodist religion of his preacher father would keep Canada and its world safe from any danger. The First World War shattered those idols, changing Pearson forever and setting him adrift. Exposed as an airman and soldier to the squalour and cruelty of war in Europe and Asia, he suffered a nervous collapse. John English, his biographer, concludes that he "stumbled for a while in the new terrain, and his breakdown of 1918–19 deeply affected him, forcing him to limit his range and to resist emotional ties with others and with faiths or ideologies that demanded intense commitments." He was now a cool young man, apparently devoid of obsession, eager to please and easily underrated. He covered his ambition and keen intelligence well.

Diplomacy was Pearson's natural craft. After postwar stints at an American meat-packing firm, at Oxford University, and at the University of Toronto as a history professor, "Mike" (a name he picked up from his Royal Air Force squadron commander, who thought "Lester" unwarlike) joined the Canadian Department of External Affairs in 1928. He rose not quickly but steadily in the tiny ministry, serving at the League of Nations in Geneva, at Canada House in England, and in Washington, where he ended the Second World War as ambassador. In 1946 he became the department's administrative head, or undersecretary, and in 1948 left the bureaucracy to enter politics. He was immediately named the Canadian foreign minister.

His snobbish colleagues in External Affairs thought that becoming "a mere politician" was demeaning. However, Mackenzie King, a shrewd judge of political talent, had already told him that he was likely to be the next prime minister after Louis St. Laurent. The Liberals, after all, were going to govern forever. Soon after King's retirement, he and St. Laurent formed an unbeatable combination. Pearson supplied the energy and ideas, St. Laurent the political clout and sober judgement.

Pearson was a hard-working and active foreign minister, with an infectious charm that worked best one on one and a wide network of international contacts. In the late 1950s the world was split into two implacable Cold War camps, each with enough destructive power to annihilate the other. Fearful of the Soviets but also sceptical of the Americans, Pearson contributed patience, tolerance, flexibility, and a sense of proportion to the formation of the North Atlantic Treaty Organization, the building of a multi-racial Commonwealth of Nations, and the resolution of the Korean War.

In 1956 Pearson engineered a United Nations peacekeeping force to calm the fires of the Suez Crisis in the Middle East, after Egypt nationalized the Suez Canal and Britain and France (with Israel's help) tried to take it back by force. Pearson won the Nobel Peace Prize for making "aggressive forces yield without resorting to power." The word *Pearsonian* began to creep into the language to describe Canada's enlightened engagement with the world. He was the symbol of a Canada that had shaken off the doldrums of the Great Depression and emerged from the Second World War as a country of the front rank. Canadians, particularly the young, looked up to the fresh-faced Mike as their ideal.

With the Nobel medal in his pocket, he was unbeatable in the race for the Liberal leadership after St. Laurent's unexpected defeat by John Diefenbaker in the election of 1957. Pearson's career as leader of the opposition started badly, however, with his demand that the Conservatives vacate office and return power where it belonged—to the natural governing party. Dief heaped ridicule on derision, and promptly called a snap election for March 1958. The Liberal war cry, "Peace, Prosperity, Pearson," was as hapless as their campaign. Dief won 208 seats. All that was left to Pearson were forty-nine constituencies, and only fourteen west of Quebec.

One of those wins, to his blunt wife Maryon's dismay, was Pearson's own in Ontario's Algoma East. "We've lost everything," she said. "We even won our own seat." So he had to stay, clawing his way back from the worst defeat in Liberal history, fighting the messianic Diefenbaker daily in Parliament.

And with what? An international superstar he might be, but he was entering his sixties, and he admitted that he found it difficult to remember "that in party politics all is black and white." He detested "the hoopla, the circus part of it, all that sort of thing. It still makes me blush." Nor did he have the public speaker's voice or the politician's instinct for exposing raw emotion. His lisp became more pronounced in front of big crowds, and what "was intended as forceful oratory," noted one observer, "came across, more often than not, as a modified, high-pitched splutter."

Yet he was vigorous and had kept the ruddy athleticism of his youth—a House of Commons physiotherapist pronounced him the fittest man on Parliament Hill. Painstakingly, he made himself over into an effective opposition leader, learning, the Toronto *Telegram* reported, to be "a party professional hitting to hurt" in the House. By 1960 Richard Gwyn, writing in *Saturday Night*, saw someone much tougher than "the boyish, smiling diplomat. He now really wants to be prime minister—something that was doubtful two years ago." He also remained "a magnet for able men." Under his influence, the party began to take on new ideas and new people, and with them a progressive tilt on issues such as health care and social security.

The Liberals, ably assisted by Diefenbaker's poor performance, moved ahead in the polls and remained there when an election was called for June 1962. Pearson had dutifully taken television lessons and discarded his old-fashioned bow tie, but very few voters were prepared to back the party because of the leader, who was still thought of as a "diplomat" out of touch with the real Canada. At the end, the Pearson team had slightly more popular support than the Conservatives. Diefenbaker, however, led in seats, 116 to 100. He clung to power.

Pearson returned to the opposition benches with momentum on his side, but knowing he would have to retire—would

LUDICROUSLY FALSE AND MALICIOUS INVENTION! THERE IS NO CORRUPTION IN HIGH PLACES.

Macpherson / National Archives of Canada C-113612

want to retire—if there was not another election soon. The opportunity came when the Conservatives disintegrated in early 1963, unable to decide on the nuclear weapons issue. Seizing the advantage, and making the decision by himself, Pearson blatantly reversed Liberal policy with an address pledging to install nuclear warheads on Canada's missiles when he became prime minister. This decision appealed to the many Canadians who believed that Diefenbaker had been breaking his alliance commitments to the United States, but Pearson's shining reputation as a peacemaker suffered badly. The Quebec intellectual Pierre Trudeau turned away in disgust from the man he called "the unfrocked priest of peace."

The Liberals began the 1963 election with a huge lead, good candidates, detailed policies, and lots of money—all tributes to the way Pearson had been running the party. But Diefenbaker performed magically in the campaign. Pearson, again unable to connect with the electorate, did not. He might be the first Canadian who had ever printed a clear image on the mind of the world, Fulford wrote two days before the election, but Pearson was "still unable, after working at it for five years, to imprint a clear image of himself on the mind of Canada." After one dispiriting speech in Vancouver, when protesters screaming "Yankee stooge" pelted him with their pea-shooters, he and Maryon vowed that this would be their last run at power. Pearson limped to the finish line with 129 seats, four short of a majority but enough to form a government.

He had made the flashy promise that his new administration would begin with "Sixty Days of Decision," bringing efficiency and resolution back to national government. The prime minister started well enough with visits to the British capital and to President John F. Kennedy, a warm supporter who had offered, to Pearson's horror, to intervene in the election on the Liberals' behalf.

The "Sixty Days" created unrealistic expectations and achieved puny returns. The inexperienced finance minister, Walter Gordon, a key party organizer and Pearson benefactor, rushed his budget and botched it badly. His ill-conceived measures to reduce foreign investment raised the ire of the business community. On the sixtieth day, with the criticisms turning white hot, Gordon offered to resign. Pearson wanted the minister to go, but would not push him out. Instead he put the onus on Gordon, asking whether he had enough confidence in himself to continue. Gordon, though bitter and wounded, never lacked confidence. He stayed.

This, it turned out, was standard operating procedure for the new prime minister. Pearson avoided choices and put off decisions. As he always had, he told people what he thought they wanted to hear. Put under pressure, as he often was by the poisonous Diefenbaker, he did what one of his ministers called a "side-exit slide," saving himself and his feelings rather than his colleagues. The Cabinet was full of strong ministers, such as Paul Martin, Mitchell Sharp, and Jack Pickersgill, and the administration had gifted advisers such as Tom Kent and Al Johnson, but Pearson could not meld them into a team. There are fights and factions and leaks in any government; Pearson's set records on all three scores.

Pearson made good on his pledge to import the American "nukes" into Canada. He regretted that he had "become a kind of a symbol for a lot of the woolly ideas people have about peace and defence." Despite a well-publicized admission that he would rather live under communism than see the destruction of the world ("I'd rather be Red than dead"), Pearson put an equal emphasis on peace *and* power. His was the last administration in the century to take the Canadian Forces seriously; he often spoke about the defence of peace, which required military might. At the same time, always imaginative and self-critical, he publicly criticized the North Atlantic alliance he had helped to create, wondering if it was still a place where Canada could influence Western policies and put a damper on American power. Almost as soon as Canada acquired nuclear weapons, he was trying to devise ways of getting rid of them.

National unity was Pearson's chief goal and "passionate interest." During Quebec's Quiet Revolution of the early 1960s, francophones turned away from the Catholic Church and towards heightened nationalism, a strong provincial government, and sometimes even separatism. Although unable to speak French well, Pearson was sympathetic to the new reality of Quebec and determined to find ways of accommodating its hopes. Shortly after the 1963 election he made good on a promise to establish the Royal Commission on Bilingualism and Biculturalism (the B and B Commission) to inquire "into the means of developing the bilingual character of Confederation."

But a talkshop was not enough. The B and B Commission

soon reported what was already apparent. Canada was passing through the greatest crisis in its history. Quebec's government under Pearson's former colleague and fellow Liberal, Jean Lesage, was on the attack, demanding that *"notre État du Quebec"* be allowed to flex its muscles in a federation that would have to change. Change or die: the challenge was stark and immediate. The prime minister responded with "cooperative federalism," a scheme that entailed more power-sharing with the provinces—though not as much as the Quebec nationalists were demanding.

Pearson could not count on his friend Lesage, as he discovered when the premier hosted a spring 1964 federal-provincial meeting on his home turf in Quebec City. The government of Canada came with a hastily concocted plan for Canada-wide contributory old age pensions. Lesage ambushed Pearson with a full-blown scheme of his own, which was more attractive to the other provinces than Ottawa's program, and a demand for a bigger share of federal taxes. A disillusioned band of Pearsonites had to scurry back home to regroup. The eventual compromise, separate Canada and Quebec pension plans with agreed standards, had advantages for both sides. But provincial power—Quebec power, in particular—was on the rise. When Pearson appealed to him to join the federal Cabinet, Lesage refused to leave Quebec.

A series of scandals uncovered by the Tory opposition eroded Pearson's public standing. They were more serious because they all involved francophones. Justice minister Guy Favreau was caught up in a sordid affair involving a drug dealer with Liberal connections and a suspicious prison escape. Pearson, who gave Favreau only lukewarm support, eventually accepted his resignation from Justice but kept him in the Cabinet, an unsatisfactory but typical compromise.

Two other Quebec ministers, meanwhile, were damaged by accusations that they had acquired furniture from a Montreal company without paying for it, while another resigned after being charged with accepting a $10,000 bribe.

The country, Pearson felt, needed distraction and an injection of patriotism. In May 1964 he announced to irate war veterans, who had proudly fought under the Red Ensign (a variation on the British flag), that he planned to create a distinctively Canadian flag. The issue dominated a malignant House of Commons for six months, with Diefenbaker and other traditionalist members kicking and screaming every step of the way. After 308 speeches had been made, Pearson forced the debate to an end and had his way. On February 15, 1965, the new flag with its huge red maple leaf was raised for the first time in front of the largest crowd to assemble on Parliament Hill since the end of the Second World War. Defence minister Paul Hellyer watched the proceedings, writing in his diary: "This will be Pearson's greatest achievement."

The government toted up impressive achievements in its first two and a half years: the flag and pensions; new funds for education, job training, regional development, and foreign aid; the Company of Young Canadians, an idealistic agency aimed at assisting community development and fighting poverty; the integration of the armed forces under a single command; more United Nations peacekeeping; a new labour code and crop insurance; the Canada–United States Autopact, a free trade zone in cars and parts; and the revision of a Canadian-American treaty for the development of the Columbia River.

Even so, Pearson wanted a majority government, so he could be "at ease." By this time he hated Diefenbaker so much that he had been willing to indulge in an attempt at blackmailing the Tory leader. Using a confidential security file claiming a breach of national security by a minister in the Diefenbaker government, Pearson all but promised that he would cover up the Chief's secret if the Conservative caucus would stop its scandalmongering. The opposition leader retaliated with an old file of his own, accusing the prime minister of being a communist, and hinted that it could easily become public knowledge. One despicable threat had been met with another. Canadian politics had never sunk lower.

Pearson had a good eye for talent, putting
Trudeau, Turner and Chrétien into his Cabinet.

Pearson was eager to dispatch Diefenbaker once and for all. Walter Gordon, directing the campaign, promised a clear victory. After his usual hesitations, Pearson called an election for November 1965 and had a twenty-point lead in the polls by the third week of the campaign. Newsworthy candidates Jean Marchand, Gérard Pelletier, and Pierre Trudeau had been convinced to do battle with the nationalists in Quebec, and businessman Robert Winters was a recruit from Ontario. The men in the back rooms were predicting 155 seats.

Then an eerie rerun of the three previous elections began: Liberal miscues, Diefenbaker charisma, and the lack of a Pearson punch. The Liberals' own pollster reported: "While few think [Pearson] is doing a bad job, most feel he is doing only a fair job." Pearson's reward was a two-seat increase to 131, still two short of the elusive majority. The headline in the Montreal *Gazette* told the tale, "Pearson Wins But Loses." He offered the party his resignation. It was not accepted.

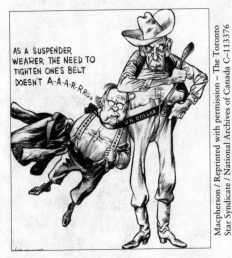

AS A SUSPENDER WEARER THE NEED TO TIGHTEN ONE'S BELT DOESN'T A-A-A-R-R-RGH

Macpherson / Reprinted with permission – The Toronto Star Syndicate / National Archives of Canada C-113376

Reined in by U.S. president Johnson.

The chaotic air of crisis management continued into the second term. So too did the good works, notable among them the implementation of Medicare for every Canadian. But the closer that program came to completion, the more inept Pearson became, delaying, seeking the support of everyone for each inch of progress, and almost scuttling the plan that has since come to be regarded as one of his greatest achievements.

He became less flexible on Quebec issues. Within Pearson's team of ministers and advisers there was a shift towards tougher federalism, with the brilliant Trudeau in an increasingly prominent position. A more demanding premier, the

Union Nationale's Daniel Johnson, replaced Lesage in Quebec City. English Canadians began to resent the accumulation of "concessions." Fear of an independent Quebec mounted, reinforced by a series of bombings and the province's forays into diplomacy. When French president Charles de Gaulle delivered his emotive cry, *"Vive le Québec libre,"* from the balcony of Montreal's city hall in 1967, Pearson rebuked him soundly in an emotional television address. De Gaulle, who was on his way to Ottawa, haughtily cancelled his official visit to the capital and went home.

De Gaulle had come to visit Expo 67, the hugely successful international exhibition held to mark 100 years of Canada's existence. Another caller there was Lyndon Johnson, who had become

National Archives of Canada C-146165

"We Canadians are fed up with your confounded meddling."

president of the United States after the assassination of John Kennedy in 1963. The United States was and remained Canada's best friend, but Pearson's relations with Johnson were a roller-coaster ride. In 1964 Johnson had been grateful to the Canadian for helping to keep the lid on a potentially explosive situation on the Mediterranean island of Cyprus. However, Pearson's speech at Temple University the next year advocating a pause in the bombing in America's war on North Vietnam was treated as a gross insult. Pearson, the famous quiet diplomat, had intervened in the affairs of another country. Johnson informed him so in a very hostile encounter, described by the Canadian ambassador to the United States as a drama that seemed at one point "to be approaching a climax of physical violence." The argument continued at Expo 67, with Pearson wanting to give peace a chance in Vietnam and Johnson rebuffing him. Pearson's biographer concludes: "Johnson let Pearson know that he did not take him very seriously. Pearson, however, took Johnson very seriously indeed. The American frightened him."

Pearson announced his retirement in December 1967 and left office the following April. His choice to follow him as party leader was Pierre Trudeau, who repaid the debt by openly repudiating Pearson's foreign policy philosophy. Mike Pearson achieved a great deal more in five years than his successor would in fifteen, but in an age of mass media, Trudeau looked and sounded better doing it. As Pearson stepped down, 70 percent of Canadians could not think of even one accomplishment of his government.

The legacy is more powerful in retrospect. Commentator Richard Gwyn, writing in 1997 on the 100th anniversary of Pearson's birth, attributed much of Canada's modern national shape to the fourteenth prime minister—the completion of the welfare state, a colour-blind immigration policy, the maple-leaf flag, a better understanding of the French fact, and the tradition of internationalism. "We are all," said Gwyn, "Pearson's children."

5 Pierre Elliott Trudeau

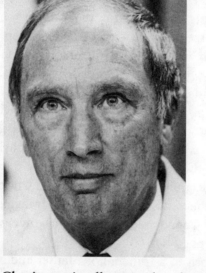

Charisma, intellect, and political courage, these qualities Pierre Trudeau had in abundance. Capturing control of the Liberal Party and the nation in 1968, he captivated Canadians and dominated their politics for sixteen years. A committed federalist, he fought all his battles with intensity, defeated the separatists, and patriated the constitution. His Charter of Rights and Freedoms changed the shape of Canadian democracy.

Born in Montreal, October 18, 1919. Prime minister for fifteen years: April 20, 1968–June 4, 1979; March 3, 1980–June 30, 1984

St. Jean-Baptiste Day in Montreal, 1968: the new Liberal leader and prime minister sat in the stands to review the annual parade on the name day of Quebec's patron saint, an event that occurred one day before the first federal election in which the governing Liberals were led by Pierre Trudeau. Separatist hotheads, well aware that Trudeau was no supporter of their position, began to pelt the reviewing stand with bottles and stones, and dignitaries scattered for cover. Not Trudeau, however. Shaking off the hands of his anxious security men, he stubbornly and courageously remained in his seat, scarcely deigning to duck the missiles whistling past his head. The nation watched on television, transfixed. Here was a new kind of Canadian leader, and the voters rushed to give him their support.

Trudeau was born to a francophone father and an anglophone mother—hence the Pierre Elliott. His father, Charlie, was an entrepreneur who started small and ended very wealthy by owning gas stations just as the automobile age exploded after the Great War. There was plenty of money to give the boy, who was shy and rather sickly, the best education possible. The flesh may have been weak but the spirit was not, and by pushing himself in every way, Trudeau eventually became a physically strong daredevil. He was no team sports player—for him it was hiking and diving, and arduous, long canoe expeditions into northern Quebec. He was no bland intellectual—he admired the great philosophers as well as the radical ideas of the times.

Initially he was attracted to the ideas of the nationalist elite of French Canada, opposed to participation in the Second World War or at best grudgingly accepting of it, and bitterly opposed to conscription. As a university student, the young Trudeau spoke at anti-conscription rallies during the plebiscite campaign of 1942, and he managed to avoid being called up for military service during the war, although he did the required training in the Canadian Officers Training Corps. To him, the war was not a matter that affected Quebec's interests, a blindness that would later cost him dearly among anglophone voters with long memories.

His life was comfortable and academic. Fluently bilingual, he travelled widely and studied in London, Paris, and Boston, emerging from it all with a law degree and a carefully honed intellect. He enjoyed trips abroad, heading off to Moscow for a Communist Party–sponsored conference on economics even in the face of Ottawa's disapproval and then writing about his experiences in the newspapers. He was in China during the Communist takeover, in the armed camp that was the Middle East, in Africa. No other prime minister before or since had the background knowledge of the world that Trudeau acquired.

But he was still a long way from becoming a national leader. He first won his spurs in politics by opposing the government of Maurice Duplessis during the great strike in the town of Asbestos in 1949, and he paid a price for daring to be against Le Chef when he was denied a position in the Law Faculty at the Université de Montréal. He dabbled in television in the early 1960s, toyed with joining the New Democratic Party, opposed Canada's acquisition of nuclear weapons, and remained a man about town and something of a dilettante well into his forties.

His self-proclaimed role was to resist the prevailing trend, whatever it was. During the 1940s and 1950s, at a time when Ottawa was centralizing power, he was for provincial rights. But once the Quiet Revolution began to take hold in Quebec, once the federal system came under assault by a group of astute politicians and nationalist ideologues who looked to increasing autonomy and, for many, ultimate independence for Quebec, Trudeau found the cause he had been looking for. In brilliant, scathing articles, he tackled head on the assumptions that underlay the *indépendantiste* cause. In 1965 the Pearson Liberals, casting about for new federalist faces in Quebec, hit upon the idea of bringing to Ottawa the "three wise men": Jean Marchand, a major labour leader; Gérard Pelletier, a prominent journalist; and Trudeau. The Grits believed Marchand was the real catch, but he insisted that his friends accompany him, so Trudeau was parachuted into a safe seat in Mount Royal. The three won and they changed the nation.

Trudeau quickly became parliamentary secretary to the prime minister and, almost at once, Pearson's policy of co-operative federalism, designed to accommodate Quebec's demands for autonomy, stiffened. Soon Trudeau became justice minister with full responsibility for the constitutional file and much else, including a reform of the Criminal Code. In this context he observed dryly and famously that the state has no place in the bedrooms of the nation. Trudeau's tough mind was on full display for a slightly shocked nation during a televised constitutional conference when he eviscerated premier Daniel Johnson. The premier asked for more powers and Trudeau mocked him by declaring, "If we could have our cake and eat it, and the candles and icing, I would be happy." Politicians didn't talk like that, and he soon became the media and academic darling.

Pearson was on the verge of retiring from office, and the

Liberal Party's principle of alternating leaders demanded a francophone. When Marchand declined to put his name forward, Trudeau, pressed by his friends, by academics who supported his views on federalism, and by an increasingly

CANADIAN FOREIGN POLICY

STOP-WORK ORDER

KISSINGER

NEWS ITEM: TRUDEAU PLANS LEFTIST STANCE FOR FOREIGN AFFAIRS.

fawning media, at last began to consider the idea seriously. He went away for a vacation to consider his decision—and met a beautiful young woman named Margaret Sinclair whom he would wed two years later—and returned to declare his candidacy. It was not quite a landslide, but Trudeau, like Mackenzie King a half-century before when the issue had been the relations between labour and capital, seemed the ideal man for the times: he was a tough federalist, the man in English

Canada's eyes to put Quebec in its place; he was perfectly bilingual; he had written a book—*Federalism and the French Canadians*—that few had read but all had heard of. At a huge Liberal convention, Trudeau wore a rose and won a tough battle against former Cabinet minister and businessman Robert Winters. Stunningly and speedily, he had captured control of the nation and become leader of the Liberal Party and then prime minister.

Quickly winning the election of 1968 with his charismatic appearance, his mastery of television, and his carefully planned but apparently improvised actions, Trudeau set out to remake government. He clamped down on the leaks that had tormented Pearson's Cabinet. He reorganized the Cabinet committee system and reviewed Canadian foreign policy, cutting Canada's contribution to NATO in half and declaring that Canada's role as "helpful fixer" was over. In effect, this change in direction was a direct slap in Pearson's face. He proclaimed his intention to create a "just society" in Canada: it would be one in which all would participate, one with personal and political freedom more securely ensured, one that protected minority rights and had more opportunities for disadvantaged regions and groups, and one that would use new techniques and knowledge to attack old social problems such as poor housing and pollution.

And then there was Quebec. Trudeau insisted that Ottawa was the Québécois' government just as much as that in Quebec City, and he set out to make it so. Québécois had no need of special status or a "distinct society." Quebec was an adult society and its people did not need special favours or privileges to face the challenges of life. What they needed was the right to compete fairly, to use their talents to the full. Under Trudeau, they did. Francophones began to rise in the civil service and they had a prominent place in his government. He put the Official Languages Act in place in 1969, a measure that entrenched the rights of francophones to their language wherever they lived and gave public servants the choice of their language of work. "Either one nation with two languages," he said, "or, ultimately, two separate nations."

National Archives of Canada C-112293

But Trudeau's efforts meant little to Quebec separatists. There had been terrorist acts in Quebec during the 1960s, militant separatists planting bombs in federal buildings and mailboxes, causing some deaths. But in October 1970 the Front de libération du Québec kidnapped the British trade commissioner in Montreal and then followed up by seizing the province's labour minister, Pierre Laporte. The Quebec government and media panicked, the democratic separatist René Lévesque seemed poised to be the beneficiary of the crisis, and student and union sympathizers filled the streets. Trudeau responded with vigour, sending troops into Montreal, proclaiming the blunt instrument of the War Measures Act, and authorizing hundreds of arrests. The FLQ responded by murdering Laporte. Trudeau, his face a frozen mask, went on television to denounce this atrocity. If opinion in Quebec had been on a knife edge, the tough federal actions and the murder combined to give Trudeau huge support in opinion polls. The crisis ended as a clear victory over terrorism and separatism; terrorism stayed dead, but separatism would emerge again.

But if Trudeau had won this confrontation, his government's slim record of legislative accomplishment, his frequently insouciant style, and his willingness to challenge critics and savage them with his viperish tongue—"Why should I sell your wheat?" he asked protesting Prairie farmers—combined to produce a minority government in 1972. The charisma of 1968 had seemingly faded. Trudeau, who had paid little attention to the Liberal Party machine up until then, now turned to the experts for help. Governing with the support of the New Democratic Party, offering popular nationalist policies and spending freely on social security and welfare programs, he restored his fortunes and won a majority in 1974.

The next years were difficult ones. The government spent public funds freely, building up deficits that mounted each year. Trudeau's efforts to find a constitutional settlement with Quebec and the increasingly obstreperous anglophone provincial governments had almost produced a success at Victoria in 1971, but that deal had been scuttled by opposition in Quebec. Now in 1976, shatteringly, the Parti Québécois and

René Lévesque took power in Quebec, capping a remarkable comeback from the ruination of the October Crisis. Lévesque's charisma was the equal of Trudeau's—and he seemed more human, more fallible, and less patrician. The voters loved him, and Trudeau and English Canada now had to contend with a government that demanded independence and sovereignty-association—but only after a referendum. The manoeuvring over the next three years was intense. Lévesque spoke in New York and bombed before an audience of business leaders; Trudeau spoke before Congress in Washington and scored a triumph, cementing the US administration's support for a united Canada. Every federal-provincial meeting was a test of wills, every international conference where France could meddle a chance for Quebec to gain a few centimetres in its battle against Trudeau.

By 1979 the government had reached its constitutional limit of five years, and Trudeau's government was tired and dispirited. John Turner, the most powerful Ontario minister, had resigned in frustration, and many others in English Canada had been turned off by the government's total fixation on Quebec. The election produced a Progressive Conservative minority government under Joe Clark, and the separatists in Quebec, preparing for their referendum in May 1980, breathed a profound sigh of relief that at last Trudeau was gone. But Clark somehow managed to lose a vote of confidence in the House of Commons and Trudeau, who had resigned as leader, was recalled. In the 1980 election he decisively rebounded from the boredom that had characterized his performance in the 1979 election and astonishingly captured a majority once more. "Welcome to the 1980s," he told a cheering crowd on election night.

His return galvanized the federalist forces in Quebec, which had been demoralized by Lévesque's charismatic appeal and Clark's mushy talk of Canada as a "community of communities." Trudeau delivered several major speeches during the referendum campaign with devastating effect and destroyed Lévesque, who had mocked Trudeau's half-British ancestors in a vituperative speech. He was capable of passionate argumentation: "The answer is NO to those who advocate separation rather than sharing," he said in a Montreal speech, "to those who advocate isolation rather than fellowship, to those who—basically—advocate pride rather than love, because love involves coming together and meeting others halfway, and working with them to build a better world." The 60 percent vote against Lévesque's convoluted and weak sovereignty-association question seemed to have put paid to Quebec independence for a generation. It was Trudeau's triumphant moment.

Trudeau's government also moved to deal with the trend in rising oil prices by acting forcefully to nationalize companies and control oil lands. The reaction in and from Alberta, which had the lion's share of Canada's oil reserves, was hostile, and Petro-Canada, the new government oil company, was scorned in the province, its headquarters dubbed "Red Square." Washington was equally unhappy, viewing this measure, like the Foreign Investment Review Agency that Trudeau's government had created, as virtually confiscatory legislation. As it turned out, oil prices unexpectedly turned downward and the government's policy, popular in the rest of Canada, was an expensive failure.

The constitution still galvanized Trudeau and captured his attention. In difficult marathon sessions he brought all the provinces except Quebec on side for a package that patriated the British North America Act, bringing the 1867 document home from Westminster and ending the residual powers held in Britain. That achievement symbolically and practically cut one of the last bonds of colonial subordination. At the same time, Trudeau's long-sought goal of a Canadian Charter of Rights and Freedoms, a Diefenbaker Bill of Rights with teeth, was entrenched in the constitution. The Charter changed the nation dramatically, empowering individuals, inserting judges into lawmaking far more than before, and providing a symbol of democracy to every Canadian. Patriation and the Charter were brilliant achievements, marred only by Lévesque's failure to sign on to the new constitution. Lévesque and most of the premiers had worked together in Canada and in London against Trudeau, but on what separatists ever after called the "night of the long knives," Lévesque was abandoned by the other premiers and Quebec

National Archives of Canada PA–141503

The constitution, patriated at last.

was "humiliated." In fact, separatist mythology to the contrary, Lévesque had played a strong hand in a grossly inept fashion and, very simply, he was euchred by Trudeau.

Trudeau's constitutional triumph came at a time of growing global tension between the United States, under President

Ronald Reagan, and the Soviet Union and its aging leadership. The Soviets had shot down a Korean Airlines 747 jet with huge loss of life in 1983, there were surrogate wars in Africa, and the Russians had invaded Afghanistan. The possibility of a global nuclear war was real. Trudeau, whose interest in foreign policy was intense, if sporadic, and who believed he had developed a special relationship with the leaders of the emerging nations within the Commonwealth and la Francophonie, decided to set out on his own crusade for peace. Carrying a list of points to ease tensions which had been thrashed out in a few weeks of brainstorming by his

National Archives of Canada C-128752

staff and the Department of External Affairs, Trudeau flew around the globe talking to leaders—Communist, neutralist, and democratic. Canadians cheered, but the world scarcely noticed. Reagan wished the Canadian "Godspeed" after talking to him in Washington, but one of his senior officials sneered that Trudeau was a leftist high on pot. Still, there was no war, and Trudeau, shrugging slightly, claimed and still claims some of the credit for that.

The peace mission was his last hurrah as leader. On February 28, 1984, he took a long walk in the snow and decided to resign. His marriage to Margaret Sinclair had failed—dramatically and in public—eight years before, but Trudeau's three sons were very close to his heart. Retirement would give him the time to watch them grow up. His successor, John Turner, would not govern for long, and Brian Mulroney, leading a Progressive Conservative government from September 1984, soon set out to try to bring Quebec willingly into the constitutional fold. His efforts, as it turned out, not only failed but revived separatism.

At Meech Lake and later at Charlottetown, Mulroney pushed and pulled the premiers into constitutional agreement. Neither agreement pleased Trudeau; both sacrificed federal powers for provincial agreement, and the aging former leader, as always ready to battle the received wisdom, took it upon himself "to remind Canadians that there is another view of Canada." He did so, speaking out loudly against the apparent destruction of his vision for the nation. What did Quebec nationalists want? he asked with biting sarcasm. "Keep giving us new powers and the money to exercise them or we'll leave. If Quebecers are offered the chance to have their cake and eat it too, naturally they will accept." This was no bargain. The Péquistes could not "be allowed to play the game of heads-I-win-tails-you-lose, or to hold referendums on independence every ten years." No country could permit that. "The black-mail will cease only if Canada refuses to dance to that tune."

Although he had been less than popular when he retired, not least in Quebec, Trudeau's occasional articles and even fewer speeches inevitably made front-page news. His old talent for vituperation had not dimmed, and he denounced Mulroney scathingly and with a vigour that belied his years. His efforts helped to kill the Meech Lake accord by stiffening the spines of provincial governments, notably in Manitoba and in Newfoundland, and his intervention during the national referendum on the Charlottetown accord was probably decisive in leading Canadians to reject the package. Trudeau's Canada survived intact, though so also did separatism in Quebec. The 1995 Quebec referendum on independence, again with a convoluted question capable of infinite interpretations, was only narrowly won by federalists—perhaps because Trudeau had been kept out of the campaign by an Ottawa too confident that the old leader's help was not needed.

In his eightieth year, Trudeau suffered the death of his youngest son in a tragic accident in 1998. His grief-stricken visage was as shattering to Canadians as was his silence, his eldest son taking on the spokesman's role. Pierre Trudeau's public career is almost certainly at an end, but he remains unique among Canadian leaders. He had a charisma that galvanized the nation, an intellect that towered above his contemporaries. Unlike previous prime ministers other than John Diefenbaker, he remained a public force for more than a decade after his departure from the prime ministership.

Joe Clark

Prime minister just before his fortieth birthday, the youngest ever and the first born in the West, Joe Clark found his minority government ending almost before it began, the victim of a disastrous decision to push forward with a budget vote he was sure to lose. In defeat he could not keep a grip on his leadership, and a long political life has been spent in an attempt at rehabilitation.

Born in High River, Alberta, June 5, 1939. Prime minister for nine months: June 4, 1979–March 3, 1980

J oe Clark's style was to have no style, Sandra Gwyn wrote in *Saturday Night* just after he became leader of the Conservative Party in 1976. "Talking to Clark, you are struck by his candour, his grave natural courtesy, and—something I've never remarked before in a politician—his almost total lack of ego. 'What drives me,' he says, 'is that this is the most interesting thing I could possibly think of doing. There is no sense of destiny about it. I distrust words like vision and grand design. I expect to do no more than move the country forward on some priorities.'"

Understatement was part of the man, yet only a part. Clark was deeply enmeshed in Conservative Party politics long before he could vote, convinced that public service was "a bed of thorns" but a high calling nevertheless. The son of the owner-editor of the *High River Times*, he was administering the University of Alberta student newspaper at the age of twenty: one of his grandiose ambitions was to establish a national news magazine. He was tall and gangly, very earnest and intense, awkward in movement, articulate but ponderous of speech, easy to under-estimate.

The view of an immense, scattered, squabbling country that needed to accommodate its differences brought his politics and his journalism together. Here were the beginnings of Clark's most recognizable political idea: Canadians lived locally, not nationally, and governments could only make the country work by recognizing that "we are fundamentally a community of communities."

Joe Clark

Clark had the conventional beginning of a politician-in-embryo. He joined the Progressive Conservative Student Federation, becoming its national president and often working alongside and competing with another ambitious small-town boy, Brian Mulroney. John Sawatsky, Mulroney's biographer, writes that "Clark devoted all his energy to debating issues at policy plenums while Mulroney concentrated on being the life of the party. Clark was high-strung, drank Coke by the case, and read widely. With his funny-looking haircut and ill-fitting clothes he was like a Tory boy scout with no room in his life for anything but politics. He was honest almost to the point of naivete."

Law school, the next logical step, was a bust. Clark could see that his 1960s generation was "soft and cynical," and he lost his way like so many others. But the mood was temporary. He tied himself to the newly elected chief of the Conservatives in Alberta, Peter Lougheed, and ran a strong if unsuccessful race for a seat in the provincial legislature in 1967. Then there was speechwriting and administration in the Ottawa office of the federal leader, Robert Stanfield.

Working for someone else was unsatisfying. Clark got the nomination for the southern Alberta seat of Rocky Mountain by outworking two men who had close ties to the riding. He was elected as a member of parliament in 1972. The kindly Stanfield had thought Clark was "too highly strung and nervous" to be a successful elected politician, but he was soon promoting Clark as leadership material. Veteran colleagues such as Erik Nielsen found him intensely partisan, "overly aggressive to the point of being objectionable," and apt to assume positions of authority he had not been given. But Nielsen became a convert. "Joe was invariably our most effective questioner: he was always well-prepared and inevitably had the government on the receiving end of some of the most effective, and often scathing criticism of its policies and activities." He had an "extensive vocabulary and mental agility" and "was never at a loss for a riposte."

There was no obvious successor when Stanfield departed in 1976. With Lougheed unwilling, and despite only four years in Parliament, Clark ran to win rather than to position himself for the future—a red Tory to the left of his party on social issues, on his way to fluency in French, emphasizing issues rather than image. He received a disappointing 277 votes on the first ballot (to Claude Wagner's 531 and Brian Mulroney's 357), but slowly emerged as the moderate wing's compromise candidate, edging Wagner on the final ballot by sixty-five votes. "We will not take this nation by storm, by stealth, or by surprise," he said in his victory address. "We will win it by work."

Compared with the flamboyant Pierre Trudeau, the media rated the new man as nondescript. His sizeable head, floppy ears, distinctive walk, and Santa Claus laugh were caricatured. He was said to be out of step with his generation, his party, and his province. His wife Maureen's decision to use her family name of McTeer rather than take his was seen as a sign of Clark's powerlessness. "Little Joe," the press crowed. "Joe Who?"

Clark emphasized teamwork, which wasn't easy. The caucus was unruly and disrespectful. The questions about his leadership were open and damaging. Prominent among the critics was the old lion, John Diefenbaker, whom Clark had helped oust as leader in the 1960s. Dief still haunted the Commons, questioning whether just any "passing Joe" could be prime minister. Jack Horner, the swaggering MP defeated by Clark at the 1976 convention, charged that he was not man enough to be a real Albertan. Horner eventually decamped to Trudeau's Cabinet. When Rocky Mountain was put out of existence by redistribution, Clark wanted the new constituency of Bow River, which included his home town of High River. So too did another Conservative MP, a pallid but determined one. Clark made an issue of it at first, but when he retreated to avoid a messy fight, his critics retorted that the leader of the party could not even have the riding of his choice. An impression was taking hold of rootlessness, a man unwelcome in his own province. Meanwhile, from outside Ottawa, Mulroney sniped and intrigued.

Clark pressed on with party organization and detailed policy preparation for the next election. In an effort to establish an international presence, he decided to take a "world tour" to Japan, India, and the Middle East. Political columnist Jeffrey Simpson's study of the period, *The Discipline of Power*, recounts the sad tale of a public relations nightmare: "He looked uncomfortable throughout the trip: wearing an eggshell-blue suit and an ascot while sidestepping the cow paddies on the earthen streets of an Indian village; asking ludicrous questions—'What is the totality of your land?'— or making ridiculous statements—'Jerusalem is a very holy city.' . . . Organizational foul-ups plagued the trip . . . Some of the accompanying journalists, devoid of 'hard news,' took to writing more about Clark's gaffes than about the rest of the trip."

The most famous of his foreign missteps was not one at all. En route from Tokyo, his luggage arrived too late in Bangkok to be loaded onto a connecting flight to New Delhi. It was innocent enough stuff, but an inability even to hold on to his own luggage became part of the public perception of Clark. He seemed too gawky and unworldly to become prime minister, especially when contrasted to the person currently in the job. Wildly unpopular though Trudeau might be, he was a sophisticate at ease with himself and the world.

169

In the year before the 1979 election, according to Clark pollster Allan Gregg, there was a substantial erosion in the leader's already shaky popular esteem. "The typical Canadian voter did not particularly dislike Clark (although overall reaction to him was generally unfavourable), or disapprove of his performance as leader of the Opposition. In fact, the average, non-Liberal voter found very little risk with Clark. Rather,

NEW YEAR'S RESOLUTION

National Archives of Canada C-137203

voters could simply not envision him as the prime minister."

This was a devastating indictment, and the Liberals did everything they could to make Clark the centrepiece of the election campaign. The Conservatives had a better issue: Canadians' thirst to rid themselves of Trudeau, who by this time was truly out of favour. At the finish, Clark stood only a few seats short of a majority of the seats in the House of Commons. Trudeau had been badly bloodied, if not quite slain, but somehow Clark remained a loser. Commentators declared that the Conservatives had triumphed in spite of their leader, and pointed to the Tories' anemic 36 percent of the popular vote, four points less than the Liberals. Gregg delivered the brutal news to the youngest prime minister shortly after the election: "It may not be an exaggeration to suggest that a national leader has rarely, if ever, assumed office with lower expectations concerning his ability to govern."

Yet Clark asserted immediately that he would push ahead, governing as if he had a majority in the House and pursuing the sometimes contradictory promises he had made to the electorate. Conservative writer Dalton Camp remarked on the leader's "clangorous note of—well—of a peculiarly petulant defiance." This attitude stemmed from more than stubbornness or a desire to prove he was not weak. There was an element of aggression and sometimes even recklessness about Clark. His model was John Diefenbaker, not Mackenzie King.

There were 211 campaign promises. Clark took their implementation very seriously, in spite of advice to the contrary, and his government sustained heavy damage as it backed tortuously away from two of its most celebrated but unpopular pledges: to move the Canadian Embassy in Israel to Jerusalem and to sell off the federal government–created oil company, Petro-Canada.

The embassy gambit was pure politics, devised by Clark in the midst of the 1979 election campaign. It was meant to be a vote-getter in a handful of Toronto-area constituencies with substantial Jewish populations. Earlier that year, while in Israel on his international trip, he was asked by the government there to support the idea. But Jerusalem was the holy and historic city of Jews, Arabs, and Moslems alike. Clark resisted, but not so a few months later, when the election turned on the outcome of a few races. Suddenly every ballot counted. He boldly announced that a Clark government would transplant the Canadian diplomatic compound from Tel Aviv to West Jerusalem. The Conservatives proceeded to do well in the targeted ridings, although whether that had anything to do with the Jerusalem promise is open to question.

As prime minister of a minority government, Clark could have delayed or let the problem go the way of most election talk. That was the advice from almost everyone, including the Department of External Affairs and its minister, Flora MacDonald. Clark pressed forward nevertheless, partly as a message to public servants that he was in charge, not them. There was a storm of protest. An Arab boycott of Canadian business was threatened. The issue began to dominate the government's agenda, and Clark's. After a meeting with five dissenting industrialists, he emerged pale and determined to search for a way out. His former boss, Stanfield, provided him the cover, reporting after a mission to the Middle East that the embassy in Israel should stay put. Clark, who had already begun to backtrack from this "mistake of tone," accepted Stanfield's recommendation with alacrity. He said that the embassy catastrophe was a scar that would always be there, "although not too large."

It was very large. Simpson considers the embassy catastrophe "Joe Clark's worst performance as prime minister." The electorate never forgot or forgave, and Clark had acquired an indelible "reputation for political opportunism and poor judgement." It also obscured a growing Clark confidence in international affairs. He had been nervous at the beginning of the meeting of G-7 industrialized countries in Tokyo right after taking power, but he found that he was the match of the other leaders. When he went to a Commonwealth Heads of Government meeting shortly after, he performed confidently.

Privatizing Petro-Canada was another promise that dogged Clark because he allowed it to. To the Conservatives and Clark, it served in opposition as a symbol of Liberal over-government and hatred of free enterprise. Once in power, Clark equated the issue with public confidence in his govern-ment, while others simply wondered at his foolhardy insis-tence on confronting a question that could easily have been ducked. Discipline, perspective, and a sense of proportion are vital in a leader. Clark allowed Petro-Canada to become bigger than its actual importance.

The people wanted to keep their oil company, and so did most of the Cabinet. Clark stubbornly insisted on another course, designed to show how decisive his government was, how it would not break its word. After a fierce Cabinet meet-ing in Jasper, Alberta, where the leader insisted on having his own way, a task force was set up to recommend how Petro-Canada could be turned into a private concern. The task force, however, produced a complicated report that was impossible to implement. A political ally, Ontario premier Bill Davis, urged that Petro-Canada be kept. In a time of rising interest rates, inflation, and energy shortages, the Liberals and the New Democrats smelled blood. "Save Petro-Canada, Sell Clark," NDP buttons sloganeered.

More than four months into his mandate, perhaps having waited too long, Clark began his first legislative session well battered by what were becoming known as his "flipflops" and against the background of serious federal-provincial difficulties. Central to the 1979 campaign had been his fuzzy "community of communities" appeal, but Ontario and Alberta, both controlled by Tory premiers, were conducting internecine warfare with the federal government and between themselves over energy pricing. Finance minister John Crosbie presented a tough budget on December 11, 1979, imposing an eighteen cent increase in the excise tax on each gallon of gasoline and diluting the campaign promise of income-tax deductibility for mortgage interest and property-tax payments.

A disbelieving prime minister was told the next day that the budget would not be approved by Parliament. The leaderless Liberals, Trudeau having resigned three weeks earlier, were solidly against it, as was the NDP. The small troop of Créditistes from Quebec had sustained the government in the past, but they did not like Crosbie's document either. Several Conservatives, moreover, were absent from Ottawa. Clark would not have a majority.

Clark refused to postpone the vote or make an effort to mollify the Créditistes. There was no public appetite for an election, he reasoned. If the opposition wanted one, the public would crush them just as they had done in 1958, after the Liberals had tried to push Diefenbaker out. The government fell on the 13th by six votes, and the prime minister instantly sought a dissolution of Parliament. He might have wriggled away with another vote, another day, but he seemed oblivious to the early December poll showing him down an insurmountable nineteen points to the Liberals. The 1980 election was a foregone conclusion. A resurrected Trudeau romped to victory, while Clark, to his credit, fought with great dignity and never showed discouragement. Addressing the caucus after the results were known, Clark accepted full responsibility for the defeat and wept.

He bounced right back as opposition leader, proud of his record of more open government and of the respect he had won among senior bureaucrats while prime minister. He had recruited talent for Parliament skilfully and had a fierce band of loyalists. However, the band of enemies and critics, never small, was growing. Clark could perform well, as he did in encounters with Trudeau over the constitution, but he was never secure. Finally, he stipulated that the party would have to give him more than the 66 percent vote of confidence he had received shortly after the election. At a 1983 convention held in Winnipeg the verdict was the same, a solid two-thirds, but short of the endorsement he had sought. He abruptly abdicated the leadership, declaring he was a candidate to succeed himself. Instead, the Conservatives chose his long-time rival and tormentor, Brian Mulroney.

Clark refused to go away. As a former prime minister with a strong following in the caucus, Mulroney could not ignore him. He served loyally and effectively as foreign minister from 1984 to 1990, although political writer Charlotte Gray, reflecting the common view that he consistently had his eye on the little picture rather than the big, did wonder "Joe Where?" A man of integrity and fervour, yes, but often unfocused, a crusader without a defining crusade.

In the early 1990s Mulroney needed Clark badly, making him the minister responsible for salvaging the wrecked constitutional talks of the Meech Lake process. He faltered where others had, but his conviction and thick-skinned tenacity were never in question. Retiring just before the 1993 election, he set off to promote the country as he had always seen it, the decentralized Canada vaguely explained by its warm and caring communities, "the nation too good to lose." He might be a noble failure, a newspaper columnist wrote, but he was "decent, straightforward, sincere and self-effacing—all the things that made him an unlikely PM, but won him respect despite his failures."

Clark opened a consulting company in Calgary, but he kept gravitating to Ottawa, eventually moving back to the capital and adding the job of part-time professor at Carleton University to his other work. Meanwhile, the Conservatives languished. Kim Campbell was humiliated in the 1993 election, and even the charismatic Jean Charest was able to win only twenty seats four years later. The Tories were struggling as the fifth party in the House of Commons when Charest was lured away from federal politics in 1998 to lead the Quebec Liberal Party. The Conservative leadership was suddenly open.

The temptation was too much for a man who had really never known or wanted a life apart from politics. Entering the leadership stakes twenty-two years after he had become party chief in 1976, he advertised himself as a man who had been ahead of his time and was now "well beyond the help of image-makers." Scepticism was widespread, but also regard and affection, evident in the media and opinion polls. "Same basic job, same basic Joe, but a new day," the headline in the *National Post* announced after he won the party vote and assumed command of the Conservatives once again. In a final touch of irony, Mulroney endorsed Clark, saying he was certain to be the next prime minister of Canada.

John Turner

With his aristocratic appearance and spectacular rise to political prominence, John Napier Turner was the golden boy, destiny's child. He had the pedigree and experience to be prime minister, but arrived on the scene too late. Eventually power was handed to him, but by then his political skills were corroded. Going to the polls too quickly, saddled with the sins of his predecessor, Pierre Trudeau, Turner found his reign was numbered in days.

Born in Richmond, England, June 7, 1929. Prime minister for three months: June 30, 1984–September 17, 1984

For nine years after he stalked out of the Trudeau Cabinet in 1975, John Turner was the prime minister from Central Casting. In articles such as Walter Stewart's "The Natural," the media kept Turner's name bright as he made his fortune in Toronto and readied himself, everybody was sure, for the inevitable return to national politics. "It's all there—the trim, exercised body, still, at 54, the body of an athlete; the face, handsome enough for a shirt ad, but not weak, dominated by a firm jaw; an engaging grin and those remarkable eyes—baby blue one minute, icy grey the next. He has the voice, the carriage, the manners, the polish, the brains. He is bilingual, charming, and hard-working. He chats as easily with tycoons as with janitors, smiles a lot, laughs a lot, and is guaranteed not to fade, rust, or drip on the carpet."

"She wasn't domineering or oppressive," Turner's sister remembered, "but Mummy believed in striving for excellence. Not for fame or money or ambition . . . but for excellence." After her English husband's early death, the accomplished and well-educated Phyllis Turner moved to Ottawa in the winter of 1933–34. She climbed (unusual for a woman at the time) to a very senior position in the public service, was courted by R.B. Bennett, and became a fixture in the social whirl of the incestuous little capital. Mother expected performance, and her son made himself into a fine student, an Olympic-class athlete, and, eventually, a Rhodes Scholar to Oxford University through painstaking application, the sheer intensity that was his hallmark. When he was sixteen, the family was catapulted into ease when his mother married a wealthy Vancouver entrepreneur. But John was already thinking seriously about another kind of life, in the Catholic priesthood. "If he can't be prime minister," his mother consoled herself, "he can always be Pope."

If politics was second choice, it didn't show. After a law practice in Montreal of a little more than a decade, he glided into Parliament in 1962, a natural at organization and raw politicking. In speeches he would give to any organization that asked, spitting them out in gruff, staccato, determined sentences, Turner set himself out as Modern Man—in tune with the revolution in communications and technology, a friend of labour, women, and citizens' rights, impatient with the "death struggle of a vanishing generation" and "the quarrels of another era." He met his wife, Geills, a Harvard Business School graduate, in his first campaign. She volunteered her computer skills to help him learn all he could about the riding, an idea that fitted well with the Turner ethic of prepare, prepare, prepare.

Impatient for promotion, he had a junior position in the Pearson Cabinet by 1965 and was elevated to minister of consumer affairs two years later, the perfect outlet for his message about remodelling and democratizing Canadian institutions. In the great debate dividing the Liberal Party over American investment in the Canadian economy, he compromised. He damned protectionism but also free trade with the United States, because "we must reaffirm economic independence if we are to maintain political independence."

Sometimes he could be quite radical, advocating free university education or a guaranteed annual income, but he was really a moderate in disguise. As one of his associates once put it, "he is small 'c' careful, not conservative." Not far from the assured exterior was a very pronounced anxiety to be liked and accepted. A lawyer friend recalled: "The insecurity showed in the way he tried to please everybody. It showed in the way he talked jock talk to jocks, and ordinary talk to ordinary people, whereas in fact he was a highly intellectual young man. I doubted if he would be able to take tough decisions that would displease people . . . But he eventually showed that I was wrong."

The media gushed. "A man of our time," Peter Newman of the *Toronto Star* called him, "born at the beginning of the Depression, highly educated, articulate, unsentimental, handsome enough to illuminate a million television screens and, one begins to suspect, intellectually substantial enough to back his image up." He was "churning the political water like some slick speedboat, discreetly buzzing the smug harbour of Ottawa's Establishment Liberalism." "I'm a reformer," Turner agreed. "I think there has to be a willingness to upset apple carts."

It was not enough to get him the party leadership in 1968, when Pearson retired. He lost it to Pierre Trudeau, who played the game of "man of our time" better than Turner ever could. "What's this guy got?" Turner wondered. Holding on through to the final ballot at the leadership convention, he created both respect and enmity in the Trudeau camp. A club was formed of the 195 delegates who had stuck with Turner to the end, and the media talked about it as the nucleus of another leadership bid.

The new prime minister gave him the Justice Department, the portfolio Trudeau had held, creating the suspicion that Turner was on a short lead. Nevertheless, he was a major force in the party now, brilliant at absorbing briefs from his bureaucrats, supple in the House of Commons he saw as a big happy family, and accomplished at building networks in the party and in the business and law communities. In half boast and half playground enthusiasm, he would describe his ministerial constituency of judges and lawyers: "I'm talking about thirty thousand legal eagles, kid, and they all know me."

With a substantial record in Justice and a careful performance during the FLQ crisis behind him, Turner became minister of finance in 1972. He did so reluctantly, as all politicians with hopes for the future do, but he skilfully managed a difficult portfolio in a time of minority government, hyperinflation, and skyrocketing energy prices. In September 1975, worn down by unsuccessful attempts to rein in wages and prices, and feeling undervalued by the prime minister, he offered Trudeau his resignation, not expecting it would be accepted. It was—and, the prime minister asked, how would Turner like to go to the Supreme Court? Or, making it worse, the Senate? Liberal Party expert Christina McCall reconstructs how Turner must have felt: "For an ambitious politician of forty-six, with a political following that outweighed Trudeau's own in English Canada, and an unbroken record as a winner, this was like a slap in the face . . . Tempers rose, sharp words were exchanged, and at the end of the interview Turner emerged without a job, facing a life crisis."

It wasn't much of a crisis. Turner quickly found high-paying work in the glittering towers of Toronto's Bay Street, and the legend of the prime-minister-but-for-Trudeau grew. However, when Trudeau resigned for the first time in 1979, Turner announced he would not offer himself for the leadership. When the opportunity came again in 1984, his family was sceptical and relented only at the last minute. It was wrong to think that he had just been waiting for the moment, that he was well prepared for what was to come; ties with the 195 Club, for example, had not been kept up, and only twenty-three of them could be found. Turner was content with the very good life he had, with its tennis and summer trips to Muskoka and the Arctic, with time for the children. But expectations, his own among them, were driving him back into politics. Wasn't this what his life had been for? "I hope you guys realize the sacrifice I'm making," he said revealingly to reporters, "and I hope the country realizes it."

Part of the motive had to be Trudeau. Turner hated what the long-serving prime minister had done to the party and the country—and to him. They had such differing views and personalities. Turner was one of the boys, a backslapper, an enthusiast, a respecter of tradition and authority. In their work together, Trudeau had let him down so often. On one

occasion in the early 1970s, Justice Minister Turner had persuaded the premier of British Columbia to support a new constitutional deal in return for a promise that the next Supreme Court vacancy would go to that province. Trudeau went back on his word and left Turner to pick up the pieces. During the Bay Street years, his criticisms of just about every Ottawa policy had steadily seeped out of Toronto. The impression was clear: he was mightily unimpressed by the Trudeau record and would do much better, given the chance. In a 1978 television interview, after some damaging Turner assessments of the government, Trudeau waved him away as he might an irritating bug. He had been the "obvious" successor for how many years? "Six or eight years, perhaps ten?"

It was far from a perfect run for the leadership. He had changed, slowed down, become complacent perhaps. In the view of long-time Ottawa political observer Graham Fraser, "Turner seemed to have lost the capacity he had been noted for in the 1960s and 1970s, of attracting and reciprocating loyalty. To those who had known him in his golden period as a minister, he seemed less civil, less sensitive; the self-assurance had become arrogance, and the unerring human touch was gone." In public he was stiff, a nervous laugh and smacking of lips making him seem awkward and anxious. He did not pick his assistants with the old sure hand.

Worst of all, for someone with Turner's competitive bent, he was unrehearsed and knew it. There was an air of running to catch up with the issues, illustrated by a reliance on cue cards. The contrast with Jean Chrétien, his chief opponent in the coming convention, was noted by the media, which had been puffing Turner for nine years. Chrétien was the natural now; Turner was trying too hard. Chrétien shot from the heart; Turner was frosty.

He was also out of touch, particularly with a party that still belonged to another man. Turner had always been a booster of provincial rights, and he wanted to send a signal that he would be a more accommodating federalist than Trudeau. However, it was impolitic to declare his support early on in his leadership bid for the recent language initiatives of the Quebec and Manitoba governments and to appear less than fully committed to a strong Ottawa role in the protection of minority rights in those provinces. The shining armour looked rusty as well when Turner allowed himself to be drawn into a controversy over how and why he left the Cabinet in 1975. Trudeau denounced him in a press release.

Turner stopped talking about the prime minister, but his leadership platform was an implicit rejection of the Trudeau program. He urged deficit and debt reduction, better relations with the United States and the provinces, and an emphasis on western Canada, where the Liberals had languished for many years. But Chrétien, who proudly followed Trudeau all down the line, had taken over as the representative of change. Turner was thought to be the candidate of the establishment, as indeed he was. Most of Trudeau's Cabinet, sensing they had a winner in Turner, supported him, and so did two-thirds of the official party delegates to the 1984 Ottawa leadership convention. He won with ease. People liked Chrétien more, but Turner was thought tougher, sounder, more competent, and better on television. When asked who was best able to help the Liberals to victory in the next election, delegates favoured Turner 63 percent to 19 for Chrétien.

Turner emerged from the convention with a lead in the polls over Brian Mulroney's Conservatives. Against his initial instincts, and following the advice of most of his lieutenants (although not Chrétien), the new prime minister called an election immediately for September 1984, rather than governing for a few months first. Everything went wrong. His new Cabinet was dismissed as simply more of the old. Insufficient attention was paid to staff and organization. The first two weeks were frittered away, and the leader changed his campaign manager half way through the campaign.

Nor was Turner sharp on the issues or clear on strategy, which kept fluctuating. He made a number of stunningly inept patronage appointments, most left over from his predecessor, and could not explain his action plausibly. Publicly, he twice patted women colleagues on the behind and seemed oblivious to the impression he gave, apologizing late and reluctantly. In going out of his way to distance himself from Trudeau, and appearing to side with his business friends, Turner alienated the loyal core of the Liberal vote. Jeffrey Simpson delivered the harshest indictment: "Seldom, if ever, in Canadian political history has a major party conducted a campaign of such sustained ineptitude."

The leaders' television debates sealed his fate. Again Turner went against his gut, which warned him not to participate, and followed the advice of his handlers instead. In the French-language debate, he was outpointed by Mulroney, who scored well with his more streetwise French and his appeal for an end to "nearly twenty-one years of uninterrupted Liberal rule." Turner, he said, was a part of the problem. After all, he was the finance minister who had introduced deficits to the Canadian economy in the early 1970s.

The English debate was crucial, and Turner's wound was self-inflicted. When he needlessly brought up the issue of patronage, Mulroney was ready, asking the prime minister to apologize for his appointment of so many Liberals to good jobs. Turner tried to put the blame elsewhere. Twice he stammered, "I had no option." Mulroney purred that of course he had a choice: "You could have done better." There was no reply. Tory Ontario premier Bill Davis said it was the most

National Archives of Canada C–133694

dramatic six seconds he had ever seen on television.

It was all but over now. The defeat was unprecedented in Liberal history: forty seats and only 28 percent of the popular vote. The leader did win his own riding in Vancouver Quadra, making him one of only two Liberals elected west of the Ontario-Manitoba boundary. Even that came at the last moment. He had been behind in constituency polls. Only the prospect of a Conservative sweep (and gratitude that he would gamble on a difficult riding off the beaten central Canadian track) induced Vancouver voters to go with Turner.

He was leader of the Liberal Party and of the official opposition for six long unappreciated years, occasioning a devastatingly titled Greg Weston book on the subject, *Reign of Error*. Turner had to fight hard to win a 1986 leadership approval vote after his former finance minister, Marc Lalonde, urged the party to replace him if they held any hopes for the next election. Then the caucus ruptured over the Meech Lake accord, Brian Mulroney's 1987 attempt to weave the Quebec government into the constitution. Turner supported Meech Lake, which meant more sharing of federal government powers with the provinces. He had been arguing for that concept since early in his career, but it flew in the face of Trudeau Liberalism. Meanwhile, Chrétien, never reconciled to Turner as party chief, had left the House of Commons and was writing his hugely popular memoirs. He took the position of leader-in-waiting, which Turner had once held.

Turner had only one period of real redemption, the debate over the Canadian-American Free Trade Agreement. Opposing the FTA, he got his old fire back and sent the Conservatives scurrying for new arguments as he repeated ones he had believed all his life. In October 1987, the day after the bulky document was made public, Turner told the Commons that he would tear the agreement up when the Liberals took power. "We did not negotiate the deal, we are not bound by the deal, and we will not live with this deal." Anti–free trade fighter Rick Salutin, like a lot of the left, saw Turner as a captive of the corporate elite who had become transformed: "Within minutes, it seemed, he had digested the agreement and all its implications. He waved the summary of the text as though it was growing from his palm. He seemed reborn. No more stammers, confident, on solid ground." He called it "the cause of my life," and people believed him.

Turner had the Senate, still controlled by Liberals, force an election by holding up approval of the FTA. The prime minister was happy to oblige. "This guy's gone. He's finished," Mulroney said of Turner. Given his opportunity, the Liberal leader declared during the television debates that Mulroney had sold Canada out, reversing more than a century of heroic resistance to American power. Free trade would reduce Canada "to a colony of the United States, because when the economic levers go, the political independence is sure to follow." Implausibly, the prime minister maintained that the agreement was just a commercial arrangement, easily cancelled by either party, and repeatedly cautioned Turner to "be serious." "Well, I'm serious," the reply came, "and I've never been more serious in my life." Turner, not Mulroney, had captured the moment and its gravity.

It was sweet revenge for 1984, but fleeting. Turner could not have won the 1988 election. Business—and business money—was arrayed against him. The New Democrats split the anti–free trade vote—and attacked Turner mercilessly into the bargain. Meanwhile, he had to deal with another caucus revolt, this time a full-throated coup against his leadership, in mid-election. The final result—eighty-three seats and 32 per cent of the vote—was not nearly enough to dethrone Mulroney. But Turner had his honour and his dignity back.

John Turner's period as prime minister was cruelly short, no longer than the 1984 election campaign. He never really governed the country or had the chance to demonstrate the skills that had made him such an effective Cabinet minister. In the modern media age, the trip from being a "man of our time" to an anachronism takes only a few seconds.

Brian Mulroney

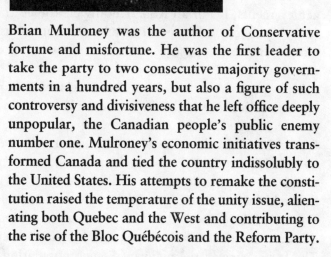

Brian Mulroney was the author of Conservative fortune and misfortune. He was the first leader to take the party to two consecutive majority governments in a hundred years, but also a figure of such controversy and divisiveness that he left office deeply unpopular, the Canadian people's public enemy number one. Mulroney's economic initiatives transformed Canada and tied the country indissolubly to the United States. His attempts to remake the constitution raised the temperature of the unity issue, alienating both Quebec and the West and contributing to the rise of the Bloc Québécois and the Reform Party.

Born in Baie Comeau, Quebec, March 20, 1939. Prime
minister for nine years: September 17, 1984–June 13, 1993

Mulroney was a revolutionary leader whose initiatives
changed the life of every Canadian. Style, not substance, brought him down. The public regarded him as high
living and uncaring. He appeared so full of self, so convinced
of his own cleverness. The overblown rhetoric was seldom
persuasive; the salesman's manner and sanctimonious plati-
tudes grated. His admiration for the United States, its leadership and lifestyle, was ripe for caricature. Canadians came to
despise Mulroney in a visceral way, according to conservative
columnist Michael Harris: "It was his fatal cronyism, his
flannel-throated hypocrisy, his stunning cynicism, his imag-
ined greed, his contempt for the people." In rating his performance as prime minister as average, despite major
achievements, historian Robert Bothwell argued that Mulroney's public deficiencies ultimately undermined his private
virtues. His very appearance "became a byword for complacent insincerity."

Mulroney's family was Irish Catholic. He was brought up
on the north shore of the St. Lawrence River in a company
town controlled by the American newspaper mogul, Colonel
Robert McCormick. Brian adored his father, who worked as
an electrician at the Baie Comeau paper mill, but townspeople
wondered how Ben Mulroney could have produced a son so
unlike himself. According to John Sawatsky's *Mulroney: The
Politics of Ambition*, "the elder Mulroney was modest and
unassuming; the son was outspoken, self-assured, even cocky.
The father viewed the majority French population of Baie

National Archives of Canada C-133700

Comeau with caution; the son saw them as potential friends. And while Ben Mulroney quietly accepted his second-class station in Baie Comeau society, Brian did not."

Politics was a way out and up. At St. Francis Xavier University in Nova Scotia, he was an indifferent student, channelling his energy instead to the debating team and the activities of the Conservative Party at both the campus and the national level. He got to know Prime Minister John Diefenbaker and worked for Davie Fulton and Alvin Hamilton, two notable Conservative cabinet ministers. He looked up to the Chief, who had proved that the Liberals were not invincible, but later participated in the Dump Dief movement, mainly because he knew the prime minister was completely out of touch with his native province of Quebec. He always said that the Conservatives could do nothing without Quebec, and he took to sending Mason Wade's history, *The French Canadians*, to friends in other parts of the country.

At the age of twenty-one, while at Université Laval in Quebec City, he was chosen by *Maclean's* as one of the country's most promising young people. He spoke to the magazine's reporters with the wide-eyed optimism of the age, inspired by the sparkle from the south of President John F. Kennedy, another of his heroes. Asked how future leaders would deal with the distribution of jobs and favours to the party faithful, he predicted drastically changed attitudes. "The young people of today," he said, "are going to strengthen the nation at the cost of partisan politics, and they are going to take a much more idealistic view of things twenty years from now than we do today." Patronage would have to go, or be drastically modified.

Nicknamed "Bones" because he was so skinny, Mulroney trained as a lawyer at Laval and went to work for one of Montreal's elite legal firms. Specializing in the management side of labour law while developing an extensive network of contacts in Quebec's business world, he was a honeyed behind-the-scenes influence in Conservative circles while catching the public eye as a hardhitting member of the Cliche Commission on violence and corruption in the construction industry.

Just thirty-seven years old, Mulroney ran for the national Conservative leadership in 1976. His was a slick operation, well financed by business friends, but delegates to the Ottawa convention wondered if he had substance to match the glitter and worried about electing someone who had never held political office. His oratory seemed programmed, an imitation of Kennedy with the mannerisms and cadence but not the flair, and his major address was unsuccessful in dispelling the misgivings. He led the balloting early on, but when other candidates dropped out, none threw their support his way. Eventually, he finished third behind Joe Clark, his rival since student days, who was the same age and seemed likely to block his path for a long time to come. In public, Mulroney supported the new leader; in private, like many other Tories, he undermined him.

Nursing his wounds, Mulroney became president of the Iron Ore Company of Canada. When Clark astonishingly declared his position open in 1983 after a 66 percent leadership support vote, the battle between the two was on again. Just at that moment, Mulroney turned a potential embarrassment into a public affairs bonanza by deftly phasing out his company's operations in Schefferville, Quebec. His considerable political skills, in both English and French, were never in doubt.

The 1976 leadership race had been a lesson. This time the Mulroney campaign was low key and cautious, run from basements rather than boardrooms. He emphasized his Quebec roots, repeating the message again and again that the Conservatives would have to capture Quebec if they were going to rule Canada. Delegates to the Ottawa convention, many of them assiduously courted by Mulroney over the years, did not think he was the best or even the most attractive candidate. Nevertheless, he was able to convince them that he had the right mix of business acumen, social conscience, and commitment to individual enterprise. Above all, he was judged a potential winner in a party of losers. On the fourth ballot, Mulroney defeated Clark: 1,584 to 1,325.

As the new leader of the opposition, Mulroney quickly mastered the House of Commons, showing particular skill in keeping his members in line over the divisive question of French-language rights in Manitoba. He threatened and cajoled and was flexible when he needed to be, all the while insisting on the principle of bilingualism. He told a journalist that he was in Parliament "to protect the fundamental rights of the Canadian people and to provide my party with a vision of the country that will reflect at all times a faithful image of my thinking and my heritage." "Hell," he said referring to his Manitoba MPs, "what are these guys thinking about? That's what being an opposition party for too long does to you, you tend to confuse prejudice and policies. Bilingualism is the goddam law of the land. We are either for it or against it, and as long as I'm leader we are for it." As Sawatsky says, Mulroney "had pulled the Tory caucus together in a way not seen since the early days of Diefenbaker."

He brimmed with optimism and confidence when a federal election was called for September 1984. Initial polls showed him down eight to ten points, but he campaigned superbly, promising to improve the recession-stricken economy and heal the huge rifts between the provinces and the federal government, and between Canada and the United States. Reporter Val Sears recalled that the "basis of his pitch was simple—Liberal-bashing, NDP-kicking—and a healthy dose of patriotism. There was also the vital and recurring theme of change . . . the leitmotif of the entire race." Mulroney set off to slay the complacent government party with a commitment: "We will be offering new people, new ideas and a new approach to government. We will be offering change." He also offered, memorably, "jobs, jobs, jobs."

Mulroney was vigorous and young and well prepared. Sears wrote that the Tory leader had carefully laid the groundwork for a buttery-smooth run at power. "He had trotted back and forth across the country—25,000 miles in all, trying out his speech in various forms in church basements and school auditoriums." He and key organizer Norm Atkins "had worked on his strengths, repaired his weaknesses. He and his perky wife, Mila, had shaken a thousand hands" even before the election was called. She was one of his great weapons. As Kim Campbell observed in her memoirs, the Mulroneys were a formidable couple. "She was an advocate for his comfort, a smoother of ruffled feathers, and a constant source of loving encouragement."

Mulroney ran in Quebec, in the riding that included Baie Comeau and Schefferville, a decision that took some courage because the Liberal candidate was popular and the province a Grit stronghold. He won the French-language leaders' debate and that shifted perceptions. Biographer Ian MacDonald notes: "He had begun to establish himself in the minds of Quebec voters as a favourite son and prospective prime minister." His easy, colloquial French was an advantage in his home province, and so too was the support of nationalists who wanted to rid themselves of the Liberals.

Mulroney pilloried Liberal leader John Turner for ramming through an obscene pile of patronage appointments, the bulk of which had been arranged by Trudeau on his political deathbed. In a dramatic moment in the English-language leaders' debate, Turner insisted he had no option but to go along with Trudeau's last-minute dash to the pork barrel. "You had an option, sir," Mulroney solemnly replied. "You could have said, 'I'm not going to do it. This is wrong for Canada. And I'm not going to ask Canadians to pay the price.' You had an option, sir, to say no, and you chose to say yes, yes to the old attitudes and the old stories of the Liberal Party."

It was the campaign's defining moment, and Mulroney kept reminding the electorate of Turner's gaffe. "The devil made him do it," he would snort in speech after speech. Earlier on in the campaign he had been quoted by a reporter saying that, if he'd been offered one of the Liberal jobs, "I'd have been in there with my nose in the public trough like the rest of them." He apologized profusely for that, saying he was sorry to have "joked" about such a serious issue and "very much regretted" the mistake. His party would overhaul the entire patronage system if elected. He later said repentance was a matter of political instinct, showing the difference between him and Turner, who was reacting to danger in slow motion.

The Mulroney Conservatives took 211 of 282 seats, the most that had ever been won by a political party in a Canadian federal election. The magnitude of his victory was a complete surprise, especially in Quebec, where the Liberals crumbled and Mulroney captured fifty-eight of seventy-five ridings. A member of parliament for only a year, never having served in Cabinet, Mulroney was in undisputed command of his party and the country.

He was not afraid of Americans—quite the contrary—and was more at home with them than any previous prime minister. What better neighbours could Canadians have? In his words, "Good relations, super relations" with the United States were at the top of the agenda. Eight days after his election victory, he was at President Ronald Reagan's side in Washington with a pledge to dismantle the Trudeau policies on energy and investment that had angered the United States. On St. Patrick's Day 1985 the prime minister welcomed fellow-Irishman Reagan to a sunny Quebec City, where they agreed to study the possibility of Canada–United States free

Aislin / *The Gazette* (Montreal)

trade. Sophisticates cringed when Mulroney sang "When Irish Eyes Are Smiling" at the finish of a nationally televised night of entertainment, while his detractors twitted him for the chumminess of it all.

Mulroney had raised very high expectations, and disappointments were inescapable. He was quickly caught up in expensive indulgence and the trappings of power, and in the patronage he had eloquently criticized. There was no easy solution to the unemployment problem. The prime minister promised to cut the huge federal deficit, an apparently popular move, but not if it affected the benefits Canadians saw as their right. When the Conservatives tried to scale back increases in seniors' pensions, they triggered accusations that

Mulroney had betrayed what he had called during the election a "sacred trust," the government's commitment to the social safety net that protected all Canadians. A francophone woman voter confronted him directly on Parliament Hill: "You lied, Charlie Brown." He backed away from change.

On the first anniversary of the government's election, *Maclean's* concluded that Mulroney was wearing his crown uneasily. The image had formed of a prime minister "crippled by indifference or indecision." Voter approval plummeted. In late 1985 a poll demonstrated the widespread belief that Mulroney had reneged on his election promises. After two years in power, 60 percent of Canadians wanted him replaced.

As promised, Canadian unity was a preoccupation. Energy agreements were signed with Newfoundland and Alberta, and discussions opened to achieve Quebec's signature on the 1982 constitution, which that provincial government had never accepted. With Mulroney presiding, the talks culminated in the 1987 Meech Lake accord, a controversial undertaking that declared Quebec a "distinct society" and conferred major new powers on all the provinces. He was given high marks in some circles for brokering a historic bargain, but the advocates of a strong federal government were outraged, not least Pierre Trudeau, who was vitriolic in denouncing the deal.

Meech Lake did nothing to enhance the prime minister's reputation. Three months after the signature of the agreement, the government had the confidence of scarcely more than a quarter of the population, an unpopularity largely put down to the boss. Mulroney was viewed as deceitful, untrustworthy, and permanently on the make. Despite having ostentatiously criticized patronage, and promised to do better, he rewarded his friends shamelessly. When every Conservative in Canada had a government plum, he once carelessly told reporters, then Liberals might get a crack at federal largesse. Scandals further undermined his appointments, and there were embarrassing resignations from Cabinet. He looked like a one-term prime minister.

Free trade changed all that. Going against his pronouncements in the run to the leadership, when he said Canadians would be crushed by their elephantine neighbour in such a deal, Mulroney took the decision to pursue an agreement with the Americans almost alone. He wanted it badly, to deliver on his "jobs, jobs, jobs" promise from the 1984 election and put

Macdonald, Diefenbaker . . . and Mulroney.

an end to punishing trade disputes with Washington. Brutal negotiations produced stalemate, then a complete breakdown, but eventually success, just under the wire of the American deadline. The Free Trade Agreement fell short of Mulroney's original bottom negotiating line, for example in the area of dispute settlement, but no one could mistake the FTA's size and comprehensiveness. North American tariffs would be wiped out over a ten-year period. On January 2, 1988, the prime minister signed the bulky document in his Ottawa office on Parliament Hill while his friend Reagan did the same at his ranch in Santa Barbara, California.

The FTA presented an opportunity to win another election when the Liberal-dominated Senate blocked approval of the required legislation. Mulroney's simple strategy, which worked smoothly at the beginning, was to divide the anti–free trade forces between the Turner Liberals and the New Democrats while winning the support of the 50 percent of Canadians who favoured the agreement. Turner put Mulroney on the defensive for a time, but Mulroney fought back hard in the remaining days of the campaign. In the end, with the Liberals fading and backed massively by the business lobby, the prime minister won easily. He took 170 seats, the first leader since Louis St. Laurent to achieve two majority governments in a row. Whatever its risks, free trade had required political courage of a high order. Mulroney deserved the return on his wager.

Meech Lake and free trade were favoured in Quebec, where Mulroney increased his support. But Meech was a ticking time bomb. In order to be implemented, it needed unanimous acceptance by the ten provincial parliaments within three years of the premiers' signature of the agreement. That had looked straightforward enough at first, but new governments in Newfoundland, Manitoba, and New

Brunswick had serious reservations. In the summer of 1990, after a lengthy federal-provincial meeting held as time was running out, Mulroney was close to putting the agreement together again. He then gave a reckless interview, revealing to reporters that he had deliberately put the premiers in a corner by waiting until the last minute to meet, hoping to force a settlement. He admitted to "rolling the dice" for Canada's future.

In the event, Meech Lake did not get the backing of the Manitoba or Newfoundland legislatures, but the prime minister got most of the blame. A Toronto newspaper slammed his "deception and sleazy tactics." Southam News columnist Don McGillivray declared that history would find Mulroney mainly responsible for the failure of the Meech Lake accord. The "precise turning point" had been "the publication of Mulroney's boast that he had engineered the timing of the marathon seventeen-day first ministers' conference. The cynical, manipulative tone was as offensive as the prime minister's claimed strategy." Mulroney's protégé and Quebec lieutenant, Lucien Bouchard, left the government and formed the Bloc Québécois. At the other end of the spectrum, the new Reform Party was given a powerful boost.

After a pause of collective funk, the government tried again. Mulroney and Joe Clark, one of his most successful ministers, engaged in an elaborate exercise in constitutional surgery called the Charlottetown process. The premiers were all persuaded to come along, but Canadians were not. A national referendum, held at the end of 1992 to counter the criticism that no one was listening to the people, decisively defeated the measure. Mulroney's public standing, at record lows, played its unmistakeable role in the humiliating rejection of Charlottetown.

Mulroney continued to put his activist stamp on the economy. Despite a crippling recession in the early 1990s which revived anxieties about the effects of free trade, he pushed ahead with negotiating the North American Free Trade Agreement, extending the FTA into Mexico. As part of his program of privatization, the government sold Air Canada to the private sector, adding it to a number of national institutions that were

The Mulroneys and Governor General Jeanne Sauvé greet Pierre Trudeau.

no longer to be government controlled. The tax system was renovated, and the GST was levied on a wide range of goods and services. Every time citizens paid the 7 percent tax, or had to collect it, they were apt to think of Mulroney, and not in a kindly way, even though the GST was a substitute for a hidden manufacturers' sales tax that had long been there.

The gregarious Mulroney personality was well suited to international diplomacy. He transformed himself into a polished performer and coalition-builder in the G-7 of leading industrial countries, and in the Commonwealth, where he became known as a vocal opponent of South Africa's war against its black population. British prime minister Margaret Thatcher was no fan, but close relations were cultivated with France's François Mitterrand, India's Rajiv Gandhi, Russia's Boris Yeltsin, Germany's Helmut Kohl, and America's George Bush.

"Brian became an important part of my own policy process and we would talk frequently on the phone or in person," Bush recalled. "Brian demonstrated it was possible to be both a strong leader for Canada and a true friend of the United States." In 1991 the Canadian Forces were a part, although a small one, of the Bush-led Persian Gulf War against Iraq. In the aftermath of the Cold War, he took the lead in calling for a more interventionist United Nations in a world where "the interests of nation states and the imperatives of geo-politics must be subordinated to the interests and well-being of people." A good citizen would break into a neighbour's house to prevent family violence; if need be, the international community ought to smash down borders to stop human tragedy. Mulroney's Canada supported peace efforts in the former Yugoslavia and all over the world, reinforcing its reputation as the world's top peacekeeper.

Success abroad was no answer to a damaged reputation at home. Like Trudeau, Mulroney clung to power too long, and it was difficult for his successor, Kim Campbell, to stake out an independent path. He departed the scene only months before the 1993 election, which all but destroyed the Conservative Party.

Mulroney stayed on the list of the unforgiven for years after his retirement as leader. It was as though he was responsible for every Canadian sin and problem. A book about the "crime, corruption and greed" in the Mulroney years, Stevie

Cameron's *On the Take*, sold over 100,000 copies; Cameron had no evidence of any wrongdoing on Mulroney's part, but the book slyly hinted that he was up to no good. In 1995 the Royal Canadian Mounted Police accused him of taking kick-backs on the sale of Airbus planes to Air Canada while prime minister, and the media—and Canadians—jumped to the conclusion that he was guilty. It took more than a year, and a legal action against the government of Canada, to win an apology and his $2 million costs from the minister of justice.

A half-decade after leaving office, he was made a Companion of the Order of Canada, occasioning protests from coast to coast. With Airbus behind him and the publication of William Kaplan's searching examination of the whole sad affair, *Presumed Guilty*, Mulroney began to emerge from self-imposed exile. In speeches and newspaper interviews he defended his government's record, arguing that imitation was the sincerest form of flattery. Hadn't the Chrétien Liberals adopted his most important policies?

Kim Campbell

Pioneering woman politician and specialist in the unorthodox, Kim Campbell was the first woman prime minister of Canada, the first from British Columbia, and the first born after the Second World War. But her inexperience and shallowness became all too apparent. After initial flash and flair she fizzled, governing for a scant 132 days before a crushing defeat in the 1993 general election reduced her party to two seats in the House of Commons.

Born in Port Alberni, British Columbia, March 10, 1947. Prime minister for four months: June 13, 1993–October 25, 1993

After her punishing defeat in the 1993 campaign, it was suddenly hard to remember the virtues that had propelled Kim Campbell to the top and so fast—the determination, the exuberance, the gregariousness, the fluency, the frankness, the sharp wit and brain. Not untypically, Angelika Sauer of the University of Winnipeg concluded that Campbell had only two political achievements to show for her short, unhappy premiership. She had proved that a woman could be prime minister, and that a woman, too, could be incompetent.

Avril Phaedra Douglas Campbell began to call herself Kim at the age of twelve, after her mother escaped a difficult marriage. Campbell remembers feelings of shame and freakishness at her mother's leaving: "The truth is that girls without mothers *are* freaks." The divorce of her parents toughened her and pushed her towards what she called "compensatory over-achievement." A sense of the powerlessness of women shaped her early experiences. Her mother had taught her the word *misogynist* at a young age. A woman had to be twice as good as a man to succeed. Fortunately, that wasn't difficult.

By high school, she was thinking big: becoming the first woman secretary general of the United Nations was briefly her goal. At the University of British Columbia she tried theatre and operettas as well as campus politics, where she was elected the first woman president of the student council. She fought the battles of the 1960s with unshaved radicals, developing a conservativism that set her apart. "I sympathized with the social concerns of campus activists, but I couldn't accept the leftist dogma."

Easily distracted, she failed second-year university. But her marks at the end were good enough to get into the celebrated London School of Economics. In 1972 she visited the Soviet Union, the subject of her studies. The repression and bureaucracy repelled her, even though she admired the Russian people. She returned to Vancouver with a husband, a Canadian professor nearly twice her age, but without the doctorate that had been her goal in England. University teaching jobs followed, but never a permanent academic appointment. She was victimized because she was a woman, she claimed, ignoring the fact that she never finished the PhD, the union card of college teachers, nor did she publish in her area of expertise.

She moved on, beginning law school in 1980 and launching a political career. As the high-profile chair of the Vancouver School Board, and with her marriage breaking apart, she promoted education for the gifted, pushed cost-cutting, and fought a teachers' strike. Bill Bennett, the Social Credit premier of British Columbia, liked what he saw. Campbell was one of his candidates in the 1983 election. He won but she lost, and after practising law briefly she was named executive director of the Premier's Office in September 1985. She married again; that, too, did not last.

"Kim has always wanted to be a politician," a friend once reported. "And she's very aggressive about achieving her goals." Against the odds and the advice of her friends, she ran for the Socred leadership when Bennett retired in 1986. She got merely a handful of votes at the convention. Worse, she made an enemy of the showy winner and new premier, Bill Vander Zalm, with her blunt warning that "charisma without substance is a dangerous thing." It "raises expectations that cannot be satisfied," she said. "Then come disillusionment

Kim cuts a rug.

and bitterness." Though elected to the legislature later that year, she had ensured that she would get nothing from "the Zalm."

Campbell, it was becoming clear, adored risk and variety. Restless by nature and feeling under-utililized, she jumped again in 1988, this time to national politics as a Conservative. Galvanized by free trade, which she thought would bring prosperity to British Columbia, Campbell won a hard fight in the riding of Vancouver Centre. Her ease on the platform made her an attractive and much-sought-after party advocate. Within a year as an MP, she was in the Mulroney Cabinet as the junior minister for Indian affairs and northern development. Mulroney wanted to promote women, and

Campbell had shown that she was tough, articulate, and bilingual.

In early 1990, after no real time to prove herself in Indian affairs but running on the fumes of pure momentum, Campbell received a startling promotion, becoming minister of justice and attorney general. The portfolio had always before been held by men, often very grey and silent ones, and she had scarcely practised law herself. She waded courageously into controversy, championing tougher gun-control legislation (after the slaughter of women engineering students in Montreal), stricter standards for the prosecution of rapists, and the regulation of abortion, except when a woman's health was at risk. The list of admirers was growing.

There were also detractors, particularly in women's groups, who viewed her as abandoning them on abortion and gun control, a politician willing to compromise her principles for political advancement. An apparently revealing photograph, showing her holding her lawyer's robe in front of bare shoulders and attracting attention to the "Madonna of Canadian politics," can hardly have helped. Campbell had women's issues at the forefront of her concerns at Justice. "I was raised to be a feminist," she told the Commons early on in her term, "and I'm not shy about promoting the feminist perspective." But she was a feminist with a difference, an individualist who insisted that "we can only live our own lives; I can't speak for all women." Was she trying to have it both ways?

Bright, energetic, and novel, Campbell had transformed herself into the most striking politician in the land. Mulroney appointed her to National Defence and Veterans Affairs at the beginning of 1993, again the first time a woman had held the job. With the prime minister set to retire, Campbell was the clear favourite to succeed him. "Who needs a leadership race? I'll just stage a military coup," she joked to the press. "Don't mess with me. I've got tanks."

The election of Bill Clinton as president of the United States was fresh in people's minds. As Richard Gwyn of the *Toronto Star* put it, "The Clinton envy factor was important: Kim was our baby-boomer." Party elders such as Joe Clark and Michael Wilson were unwilling to stand against her, and her only real rival was thirty-four-year-old Jean Charest, the environment minister. Charest was the better campaigner, which should have set off more alarm bells than it did, and Campbell was sidetracked by media criticism of her handling of the murder of a Somali teenager by some of her peace-keeping soldiers. She had the party bosses and a superior organization, however, and they delivered a clear victory at the June 1993 convention—but not before Charest had made real inroads.

She was now prime minister, and she started well with a considerable reduction in the size of the Cabinet and a massive reorganization of government. Journalist Charlotte Gray reported that "she hit record levels of popularity . . . as she crisscrossed the country. In those balmy days, she looked so prime ministerial. At the Tokyo meeting of the seven largest industrial powers, when she was the only woman among the dark suits, she radiated the dignity and self-assurance shared by those at the pinnacle of power. She seemed to offer a new kind of politics: candid, straight-talking—and female." All the while she demonstrated a personal frugality much in contrast to the high-spending Mulroneys.

With the Conservatives late in the fourth year of their mandate, an election had to be called soon to avoid the impression of a government running from the people. When it came in September and October, the burden of her deeply unpopular predecessor proved enormous: Campbell was

Donato / *The Toronto Sun*

dismissed as Mulroney in a skirt by Liberal Sheila Copps. The Chrétien Liberals performed smoothly, and regional parties in the West and Quebec sapped the government's strength.

Campbell herself never found her stride. She frequently spoke without tact or sufficient thought and started to battle the media—usually a losing proposition. On one occasion, exasperated by a reporter's question, she asked him if he needed a hearing aid. Another time she seemed to say that elections were not the time to discuss serious issues, an impression she did not correct. "It was a disastrous error of judgement" not to apologize, she admits in her often angry memoir, *Time and Chance*. The focus of her campaign was jobs, growth and deficit reduction, but she was not able to get that message across. One press conference remark got interpreted as meaning that she didn't think unemployment (then at over 11 percent) would be "way down" until the turn of the century. She was inexperienced in the little lies of politics.

Campbell suffered the greatest electoral defeat of any prime minister in Canadian history, finishing with only two seats in a House of Commons of 295. Neither one was hers, so she was a leader without a place in Parliament. She had been destroyed, and Charest was in the wings. Her early resignation was inevitable.

Although it probably helped at various points in her career, there can be no doubt that she paid a heavy price for her gender. As Gray wrote in a sympathetic article in *Chatelaine* magazine, Campbell broke the rules of contemporary Canadian politics. The candidate should be able to boast a sunny nuclear family. There ought to be a neat, steady career path, preferably with a touch of rags-to-riches, as in Mulroney's escape from Baie Comeau or Chrétien's rise out of Shawinigan. Long service in the party counts, with the network of contacts that accompanies it. But Campbell was twice divorced, with an unconventional résumé and little party experience. Only nine years before she had been a local school trustee in Vancouver.

Besides, wasn't she aggressive and arrogant? Hadn't she conveyed the impression of a bossy and patronizing intellectual with a sharp tongue? These qualities were much easier to take in a man than a woman, who was supposed to exude charm, not thrust. Campbell was branded by columnist Allan Fotheringham as out for power, "a sharp-tongued mini-Thatcher with an alarming ability to leap wherever ambition leads her." Campbell said, rightly, that women's "frontal lobes have always been accepted . . . but the bodies and the lifestyles and the gender-specific aspects of our personality have not."

Kim Campbell failed the test of the campaign, the only significant challenge of her premiership. Perhaps the Conservatives had been bound to lose all along, but the magnitude of the defeat lay squarely at her door. The charisma faded quickly and the public decided the substance was not there.

Jean Chrétien

Rough-and-tumble populism at the ready, he arrived in office with experience in every major federal ministry and a reputation for honesty and integrity that seemed unshakeable. Chrétien's first term was mainly notable for efficient deficit-cutting and an almost disastrous Quebec referendum, when the country barely held together. Yet, with the opposition divided and his personal popularity intact, he sailed resolutely on, winning re-election in 1997 and maintaining a high level of public trust.

Born in Shawinigan, Quebec, January 11, 1934. Prime minister from October 25, 1993–

Joseph-Jacques-Jean Chrétien, the son and grandson of staunch Liberals, attended his first party leadership convention as a youth delegate in 1958. He supported Paul Martin, the father of a future finance minister, not the wildly popular Lester Pearson. It wasn't that Martin was the better man; rather, that Pearson's victory was a foregone conclusion. When Chrétien saw that Martin was the underdog, he said, "Goddamn it, I'm going with him."

The twenty-four year old was finishing a Université Laval law degree and about to embark on a successful practice back home in the Quebec mill town of Shawinigan. Still, he viewed himself as a rebel and an outsider, and perhaps always would. He was a product of the free-thinking and anti-establishment Liberal tradition that anchored his huge working-class family, but also of a difficult childhood made worse by a younger brother who consistently outshone him and a deafness compounded by a facial paralysis, causing him to talk noticeably out of one side of his mouth. "Some people find it hard to believe," he said after more than fifteen years in Ottawa as an important Cabinet minister, "but I've always had an inferiority complex." "Jean's a fighter," a good friend added. "He's got to win."

Chrétien intended to enter politics when he was forty. But in 1963, at the age of twenty-nine, he ran his first campaign— smart, determined, and dirty, in sympathetic biographer Lawrence Martin's estimation—against a favoured sitting member of parliament, winning by 2,000 votes. He arrived on

215

Parliament Hill in Ottawa thinking of his dead mother and demanding father, and with his political convictions well set. He was a fiscal conservative, a social policy liberal, and a spontaneous federalist—good credentials for advancement at the national level, even if he did not have much English.

A powerful friend helped. Lester Pearson's finance minister, Mitchell Sharp, liked Chrétien's quick mind, solid political instincts, and straightforward manner. He recognized the younger man's ability to convey a simple and genuine Canadianism, his commitment to a strong national government. Chrétien achieved Cabinet rank under Sharp as minister of state for finance in April 1967 and became minister of national revenue in January 1968. He was the second youngest Cabinet minister in Canadian history to that date.

He did not much like Pierre Trudeau at first, but Chrétien prospered when Trudeau succeeded Pearson as prime minister. Early on in a six-year stint as minister of Indian affairs and northern development, his department tried and failed to end the separate legal status of Canada's first peoples. This initiative caused great disgruntlement, but his headlong energy and clear dislike of paternalism won friends. Rewarded with a succession of senior economic portfolios, Chrétien was Canada's first francophone minister of finance from 1977 to 1979. Many, Trudeau included, had their doubts about Chrétien's grasp of economic complexities, and he was badly embarrassed when the prime minister announced major spending cuts without clearing them with him first. Still, as one of his top bureaucrats noted, he had "the strength of simplicity. Ask him a question and you'll get an instant decision, and he's right more times than he's wrong."

As justice minister, Chrétien grew close to Trudeau, leading the federal fight against René Lévesque's 1980 secession

The strategist and advocate shaped his own course.

referendum in Quebec and negotiating a new national constitution. He was successful on both bruising fronts, but nationalist opinion in Quebec regarded him more and more as an outsider who had betrayed his own people. Chrétien was from Quebec, but no longer of it, in the view of the elite who controlled opinion. At the same time, his homilies about a united Canada had transformed him into something of a folk hero in the rest of the country. "I love Canada," he would say with a conviction that made crowds stand and cheer.

In 1984 he was an attractive candidate for the leadership of the party, running a very effective campaign as the "man from Main Street." At the Ottawa convention, the constituency delegates split their support evenly between him and John Turner. It was the 1,000-strong Liberal aristocracy—Cabinet ministers, senators, MPs, Liberal functionaries—who defeated Chrétien. As political writer Ron Graham pointed out, "While his style may have struck a chord in the hearts of Canadians, many of whom shared his rawness and felt his sense of inferiority, many Liberals preferred to see themselves as they often were: winners, intellectuals, sophisticates. They talked a great deal and in glowing terms about the common people, but they weren't sure they wanted to be led by one of them." In truth, "there was little common about Jean Chrétien, but he couldn't alter his style without betraying his followers and himself." On the Civic Centre podium, after Turner's victory had been announced, Liberal Party president Iona Campagnolo shouted that Chrétien may have come second in votes, but he was "first in our hearts."

That comment made it more difficult. Chrétien was personally devastated, and he never adjusted to Turner at the helm. The two men had been friendly colleagues in government for a decade under Pearson and Trudeau. In 1978, however, Turner criticized Chrétien's performance as finance minister in newsletters to his business friends. Their relationship was never the same after that. Turner was not good at regret, and Chrétien, valuing loyalty above all else in politics, had a very long memory. He was made deputy prime minister and secretary of state for external affairs in the short-lived Turner government, but not given control of the Quebec party, as he thought was his due. Instead, Turner delegated the provincial organization to three ministers, and Chrétien had to work with André Ouellet and Marc Lalonde, who thought him insubstantial and had not backed him for the leadership.

Chrétien was one of only two ministers who recommended against a snap election in the summer of 1984. Turner did not listen. When the party was smashed by the well-prepared Mulroney Conservatives, it was widely speculated that Chrétien would have done better, reinforcing his belief that the Liberals had made a disastrous error in choosing another

man. Chrétien co-existed uneasily with Turner in opposition, thinly disguising his ambition and bitterness. "No one was proud of the way Chrétien behaved after the convention," writes biographer Martin. His consolation was that people adored him, flocked to him, told him he was the one they had wanted all along. When his memoirs, *Straight from the Heart*, were published in 1985, the first edition of 27,000 was gobbled up immediately by admiring Canadians. The book eventually sold 120,000 copies in hardcover and 30,000 in paper.

Neither he nor Turner really wanted the marriage to work. In early 1986 Chrétien resigned from the House of Commons. Political columnists Dalton Camp and Jeffrey Simpson split on the subject of his future. Camp was sure he had simply gone off to make money and lie low, readying himself for another try. Simpson guessed he was probably gone forever. "He deserved a better fate, or at least a more graceful end. His popularity, indispensable to him, threatening to others, did him in."

Camp was the better predictor. Chrétien made himself wealthy as a lawyer and investment counsellor, but politics were never out of his mind. His challenge to Turner was constant, and he let it slip that he hoped the 1988 election would drive a final stake through his leader's heart. It did, and Turner evaporated. Preparing Chrétien for the 1990 Liberal leadership race in Calgary, friends and supporters such as Mitchell Sharp tried to make him smoother, more versed in the issues—but it was all in vain and completely unnecessary. Chrétien handily won the race, doubling the support of his nearest rival, Paul Martin.

Chrétien had the prize, but it didn't seem to be worth much. The leadership was won the day after the Meech Lake accord died, and his opposition to it was well known. Mulroney had given "half the country away to the provinces and the rest to the United States," he complained. Two Quebec Liberals protested Chrétien's election as leader by bolting to Lucien Bouchard's fledgling Bloc Québécois. More than ever, he was a pariah in his home province—like a truck, Jeffrey Simpson wrote, with a string of tin cans attached to its fender. Why had he not followed through on the major changes he promised if Quebecers voted no to separation in 1980? Why did he then deliver a constitutional bargain that left them out and weaker? Why had he helped sabotage Meech Lake, an arrangement Quebec favoured?

The media, meanwhile, dismissed him as "yesterday's man"—in his late fifties, a bit undignified, having no new ideas and a huge backlog of experience that suddenly seemed a detriment. That impression was reinforced by a serious operation in 1990 which left him very frail for a time. Ottawa wondered if he could carry on. His adopted son,

Michel, in trouble with the law, was on the front pages of newspapers, and reporters were taking note of the contrast between his little-guy rhetoric and his comfortable existence in the company of the very wealthy. His daughter, France, was married to the son of Power Corporation's Paul Desmarais, who was also one of Chrétien's business clients. A respected Quebec commentator, Lysiane Gagnon, exclaimed that the populist image was a sham: "Just think about his wealth and lifestyle."

Resilience is an essential characteristic of a successful politician. Chrétien just kept coming, quietly. What had always been impressive about him was feel, not depth. His wife, Aline, his closest adviser, reminded him to rely on his instincts. He let the Conservatives make their mistakes while he kept a low profile, a trait that became one of his specialities as prime minister. Even when Kim Campbell had her brief fling with popularity, Chrétien remained calm and put the emphasis on the grassroots of the party, getting ready where it counted, just as Mulroney had done in 1984. Assembling a solid team to organize his office and fashion ideas for an election, Chrétien chose Paul Martin and Chaviva Hošek to produce a careful outline of where the party stood on every conceivable issue. The Red Book was brandished by every candidate in the election of October 1993, conveying just the right impression. The Chrétien Liberals had thought things through. They were ready to govern.

Canadians were nevertheless uncertain about Chrétien. After the election was called, his pollster found that twice as many people regarded Campbell as the better candidate for prime minister. Helped by the Conservative leader's poor showing during the campaign, Chrétien slowly made progress. After the Tories ran tasteless ads highlighting the physical defect on his face, he was wounded but saw a political advantage. "When I was a kid," he remembered, "people were laughing at me. But I accepted that because God gave me other qualities and I'm grateful." That was near the campaign's end, and only then was he beginning to feel really confident.

The Liberals won 177 of 295 seats, a big majority made bigger by the splitting of the vote between the four opposition parties. At 19 percent, the Reform Party under Preston Manning had the next largest chunk of support to Chrétien's 41 percent; the Bloc Québécois became the official opposition with only fifty-four seats. More than half the Liberal caucus was from Ontario, and almost none of it to the west of Manitoba. Chrétien was the first francophone Liberal leader not to carry Quebec in a federal election.

Chrétien governed against the background of a powerful separatist threat from Quebec and a huge national debt, which was finally worrying Canadians as much as it did the international community. Authors Christina McCall and Stephen Clarkson point out in their biography of Pierre Trudeau that Chrétien set out "to answer the sovereigntist challenge by governing soberly, keeping his campaign promises as far as prudent budget-making would allow, and forging a cautious new Liberalism appropriate to the times." The new prime minister, therefore, put to one side his socially minded campaign rhetoric and administered the country as a "blue Grit" who would cut rather than expand government. The public, with diminished expectations, accepted both the diagnosis and the cure, and Chrétien profited enormously from a down-to-earth style that seemed so different from Brian Mulroney's.

Chrétien's instrument of change was Finance Minister Paul Martin, who immediately began an assault on the deficit, then estimated at almost $46 billion. In his budget of February 1994 Martin promised to bring that figure just under $40 billion over the next year. Defence, harder to justify to the public with the end of the Cold War, was slashed, foreign aid slimmed, and public servants' wages kept frozen. The second Martin budget in 1995 aimed at even deeper cuts, taking billions from transfer payments to the provinces, substantially reducing the size of government, and announcing the privatization of state enterprises such as Canadian National Railways. Arthur Kroeger, the respected former senior bureaucrat, concluded that "fifty years of activist, interventionist and, above all, self-confident government" had come to a stop. Chrétien strongly supported his finance minister's revolution, but prevented him from having his determined way on pension reform. Martin considered resignation, but worked out a compromise with the prime minister which delayed the measure. In the end, Martin acknowledged Chrétien's superior political judgement.

Later that year, the Quebec government called an independence referendum for October 30. "Separation is not in the cards for Quebec," Chrétien had assured Canadians after the Parti Québécois won a narrower victory than expected in the previous year's provincial election. He remained sanguine as the polls showed the federalist *Non* forces well ahead. Another 60 to 40 win, just like 1980, was confidently expected in the Chrétien camp. The prime minister could afford to stay above the fray; the caucus must trust him and not interfere. Chrétien spoke twice in the first weeks of the campaign, soothingly on the one hand and threateningly on the other, and all seemed well.

It was anything but. The fire-eating Lucien Bouchard had arrived on the Yes side and the polls started showing the No's in decline. On October 19, after he had spoken well to the Quebec City Chamber of Commerce, Chrétien was told that the race was even, at best. The prime minister now fully engaged himself, but was it too late? He addressed a big rally in Verdun on the 24th, promising major reforms if the No side won and committing himself to recognition of Quebec as

Referendum 1997.

a distinct society—the key ingredient in the Meech Lake accord he had helped to defeat. The next day, the second anniversary of his 1993 election triumph and with the Yes camp in the lead, he broke down in front of the morning meeting of caucus, recovering quickly but revealing how much was riding on the week ahead. He taped a television address that afternoon, appealing to the substantial number of Quebecers who really didn't want to leave Canada, but who demanded a change in the status quo.

The country teetered on the brink. On referendum night, *Time* magazine reported, "Canada as a nation went through a spellbinding, nail-biting, glacial few hours that were unprecedented." The No's edged the separatists 50.6 percent to 49.4 percent; a scant 53,000 voters out of 4.8 million had made the difference. "The 128-year-old nation of Canada, a rock of stability and prosperity, would not crack asunder. At least for now." As in any tight ballot, it is impossible to know precisely what weight any one part of the campaign carried. But Chrétien's interventions had been crucial. The turn-around began as a result of his two addresses on the 25th and 26th. A Chrétien poll-taker noted that they "gave uncertain voters a reason to come back to the No."

Another federal election was called for June 1997, when Chrétien took a gamble in going to the people again after only three and half years—and with a mixed record. True, the deficit was on its way to zero, a monumental achievement, and the prime minister took pride in clean government and "re-establishing respect for institutions." But so much of Chrétien seemed warmed-over Mulroney. The Liberals had blithely signed the Mulroney-negotiated North American Free Trade Agreement, extending the Canadian-American Free Trade Agreement to Mexico. Chrétien had pledged in the 1993 campaign to re-examine NAFTA carefully; instead, there were a few minor changes. The prime minister had also admitted that he wasn't going to abolish the Goods and Services Tax, after promising to do so.

Chrétien had said that he would establish distance between Canada and the United States, but he was almost as close to Bill Clinton as Mulroney had been to Ronald Reagan. As for the rest, Chrétien's foreign policy seemed to consist mostly of lavish "Team Canada" trade missions around the world. He talked a lot about the promotion of human rights in undemocratic countries, but he did not push the issue with countries such as China and Indonesia when given the chance.

Moreover, Chrétien misjudged Quebec during the referendum, as had almost everyone else. The government has fluctuated between a tough and a soft line towards francophone nationalism ever since, one day dispensing powers such as job training to Quebec, another challenging the province's legal right to unilateral secession. The prime minister's inability to get the English-speaking provinces to concur in distinct-society status for Quebec demonstrated how narrow his room for manoeuvre was. Too much power for Quebec was unacceptable to the rest of Canada. Too few concessions risked alienating the flexible nationalists who would be crucial in the next referendum.

The 1997 election was closer than Chrétien would have liked. Reform was powerful in the West and the Bloc Québécois still strong in Quebec, despite Bouchard's departure for provincial politics. Jean Charest was bringing the Tories back. The NDP used health care, education cuts, and high unemployment as arguments that it was relevant after all. Reform, the Conservatives, and the NDP made gains and the Bloc won Quebec again. Chrétien, however, was left standing at the end—at 155 out of 301 seats, he was the first Liberal in forty years to win two straight majorities.

In Chrétien's first term, the *Globe and Mail* recalled, governing had been relatively easy. All that needed to be said was, "Didn't you hear the minister of finance? There is no money." Now there were going to be budgetary surpluses and options. Someone had to arbitrate. Someone had to discriminate among goals. Critics insisted that Chrétien and the government were adrift. They were without a *raison d'être* and coherent policies, a caretaker administration simply carrying on.

The public did not agree. In the summer of 1998 Chrétien scored well in an Angus Reid poll on representing Canada in international affairs, management of government administration and the economy, and national unity. What was lacking, the voters thought, was sensitivity—summed up by Edward Greenspon of the *Globe* as "joking at the expense of protesters who had been pepper-sprayed by the police, linking victims of the tainted-blood tragedy to drug addicts, seeming to be happy go lucky about the fall of the dollar." But as compassion, formerly a strong suit, fell by the wayside, Chrétien suffered no damage to his standing. His popularity was astonishing.

In the Prime Minister's Office, Chrétien sat at the desk that had belonged to Wilfrid Laurier, his father's favourite politician. Laurier was a point of reference, a centrist politician with a happy face. Though disdained by Quebec nationalists as he fought the battle of national unity, he always survived to fight again. Laurier in turn inspired Mackenzie King, who preached that the supreme achievements in politics—particularly in the politics of an easily divided country—lay in preventive medicine. Cautious and conservative by temperament and experience, Chrétien embraced the King philosophy of governing from the middle, day by day, avoiding the hard choices whenever possible, making the deals when necessary. The twentieth prime minister apparently had no great abiding vision of the country apart from his passion for it, but he made very few mistakes.

Conclusion

The conclusions reached in this book may be surprising to some readers, outright puzzling to others. Mackenzie King has more often been a figure of fun in the popular media for his alleged cavorting with prostitutes and his undoubted encounters with ghosts than a powerful leader who ranks at the top of the prime ministerial parade. Fans of Pierre Trudeau, Lester Pearson, and John Diefenbaker—all with their own cadres of devotees—will almost certainly feel that their men should have been placed higher. On the other hand, some will complain about Louis St. Laurent's high ranking: Couldn't anyone have led Canada well during the dull, gray 1950s? Well, no.

Canada has had some accomplished leaders and many failures. Macdonald, Laurier, and King will always rank highly on any list simply because they were prime ministers who had to deal with major problems and did so with great skill, holding office for long periods. Their individual rankings may fluctuate, but they will always be at the top, without question.

For other leaders, distance will tell. Trudeau is clearly remembered by the public today and given almost mythological status. But among scholars there is the sense that his stock is falling. Where he will place fifty years from now is impossible to say. It will depend almost certainly on what happens to Quebec and Canada, to Trudeau's constitution, and on the impact of the Canadian Charter of Rights and Freedoms. He has been out of office now for fifteen years, but it is still too early to judge his ultimate significance. An Ekos poll conducted in November and December 1998 rated Trudeau as the most trusted Canadian leader of modern times—though, in light of his about-face on wage and price controls, to cite but one instance, this is not wholly credible. Perhaps Canadians simply forget.

Not where Brian Mulroney is concerned. No prime minister left office more despised by the electorate, and polls indicate that this attitude persists. The same Ekos survey showed him as the least trusted of recent prime ministers. But what if the Free Trade Agreement over the next decades raises Canadian living standards by expanding trade and creating jobs? If we end up with a new Meech Lake–Charlottetown agreement that replicates Mulroney's attempts at constitutional reform? Or if Canada fails to hold together? Will historians in the twenty-first century look back to Mulroney as the last prime minister who creatively tried to square the constitutional circle? Or will they view him as the leader who brought the unknown Lucien Bouchard to prominence by making him ambassador to France and then a powerful Cabinet minister who became federalism's most dangerous opponent? For all we know, Mulroney may be on a historical upswing and Trudeau on a downward slide. We can simply repeat that the historians and the public today both believe that Trudeau outranks Mulroney.

Time gives perspective, yes, but time can also change it too. In his day, Mackenzie King had such a reputation for manipulative politics that few electors wanted to admit they might have voted for him. In the 1950s, an era of prosperity and unity when the odour of his compromises still hung over the nation, King certainly would not have been the choice as Canada's greatest prime minister. Now, however, he can be seen more clearly, as a leader unafraid to have strong followers, as a politician with impeccable timing and the right instincts to keep Canadians together. We cannot know if recent prime ministers will enjoy a similar rehabilitation, but if they do, it will likely be because they learned something from the unprepossessing little man from Berlin, Ontario.

Index

Index

Index

Index